Dedication

I would like to dedicate *When Will it Happen?* to my Maine friends, especially Sarah Lawson, the dear pal who trusted my family enough to show us how to find The Lily Pond.

The parenthetic poem below is about swimming with Sarah in this special place.

lily pond

water lilies on surface calm
thick green pads like palms of trusting hands
in the middle world, each is a secret one
white pointy gleams images of stars
surrounded by such jewels we swim
across the center of this perfect pond
floating flat we become like water.

Introduction

"Life is a journey, not a destination" is a motto frequently stated by many and lived by some, especially those who choose scenic routes. The drive from Caves Valley, Maryland, to Deer Isle, Maine, is 750 miles when you take the road "less traveled by," and that will make "all the difference," as Robert Frost wrote.

The trip begins following miles and miles of white-fenced horse farms in Maryland. Next, time to pause, shut car engine off. Take time to reflect at Gettysburg's haunted battlefields. Here shadowy images are known to appear clustered near the great stones of Devil's Den.

Traveling again, beyond historic monuments and souvenir gift shops, narrow two-lane country roads enter Amish farmland. Cars slow to a trotter's speed when behind horse-drawn carriages. In the back of some animal-powered trucks, goats, sheep, and pigs peer out, looking at drivers and passengers behind.

From Pennsylvania's mighty mountains, waterfalls, parks, and honeymoon resorts, travelers enter New York's woodlands and then, far away from bustling New York City, cross the mighty Hudson River. Along this waterway, in the shadows, one might see Washington Irving's *Sleepy Hollow* character Ichabod scurry to hide with the famous dozer Rip Van Winkle by his side. Away, away from the bustling city 'burbs to the quiet shores of this rolling river.

Entering New England, one finds stone-fenced farms built in the 1700s, with "telescope" houses, barns attached by an "ell", wooden plank-covered bridges. The Green and White Mountains tower in the distance. Heading east again, one route will eventually lead to Portsmouth, New Hampshire. Midway across the Piscataqua River Bridge, the big blue and white sign greets you: *Welcome to Maine.*

Across the bridge, enter Eliot, Maine, then Kittery, but there are "many miles to go" before you arrive on the island of Deer Isle. Roll down the windows and smell the air!. You have crossed into the beginning of the journey's end. Now a six-lane highway is not bordered by high-rise towers or cluttered backyards of city homes, but by granite, tall evergreens, and yellow signs warning *Deer Crossing* and even *Moose Crossing.*

The farther north you travel, the fewer cars there will be; instead, more fields, rivers, lakes, woodlands, and farms. Until, at the top of one high hill, you'll see in the distance Penobscot Bay and The Coast.

But, even then, there are many miles before you leave the mainland to cross The Bridge onto Little and Big Deer Isle.

* * *

It was August, 1985. Max and Charles were on their first vacation to Maine. Grandma and Grandpa stayed home in Maryland. Max, Charles, Ralph, baby Carrie, Mom, and stepdad Fred lived at one end of a long, wide pasture on a farm they called "The Property". Grandma and Grandpa's house was at the other end. While Max, Charles, and family were going to be away, Grandma and Grandpa would water plants, feed pets, tend to gardens and the trout hatchery.

Fred, Mom, Carrie, Max, and Charles rode in a stocked-up van. Traveling with them in their own truck were the family's best friends: Pat and his wife, Mrs. Sullivan. Riding with them were Max and Charles's 18-year-old brother, Ralph, and his girlfriend since their preteen days, Toni. Max and Charles secretly called her "Turkey Legs" Toni, or T. L. Toni for short. Pat and Mrs. Sullivan were "The Designated Chaperones" for Ralph and Toni. Pat's four-door truck was filled with suitcases, coolers, a blow-up raft, and two Otter kayaks.

Would this trip be a vacation with an adventure?

Max and Charles enjoyed adventures, and adventures always seemed to follow them wherever they went. But should an adventure pop up in Maine, they could not turn to Grandma and Grandpa for help. Grandpa's wisdom on how to deal with "Scary" would not be there.

Pat and Mrs. Sullivan, like Fred, were teachers and fun adults. Both were fond of seeking solutions when "Scary" adventures happened. Perhaps if "Scary" happened in Maine, Pat or Fred would help the boys. Only time would tell.

Max's Journal: "Our Maine Vacation"
Arrival and the Discovery of Something Strange

Day 1: August 10, 1985. Up at dawn. 7:00 a.m. into car. Ride, read, eat, nap, eat dinner, swim in hotel pool, share room with Charles. We each have our own full-size bed! Across a living-room area, Fred, Mom, and Carrie are in the master bedroom (king-size bed, Carrie's port-a-crib, and big bathroom). Ralph and T. L. Toni stay with Mrs. Sullivan and Pat in a two-bedroom suite just like ours. Toni has her own room, Ralph on the sofabed in the living area, and Mrs. Sullivan and Pat in the master bedroom.

Day 2: Sleep-in until 9:00 (later than usual). Big "all you could eat" cooked breakfast, even made myself a waffle with strawberries and whipped cream. Then, short swim at hotel. Back into van. Ride, read, sleep, listen to background noise.

11:15 a.m. Over the bridge and we crossed into Maine. Fred blew the horn. Charles jumped awake and yelled. The Maine Visitors' Center is really neat. It has all types of free literature: maps, books, hikes to take. Around the building there's a big woods, rocks, and picnic tables. We eat a snack. Back in van; watch the country go by: huge evergreen trees and no cars in any of the three lanes on Route 95. (WOW!)

Off of 95, we passed places with funny names: Vasselboro and China. We passed China Lake and Lake George where we saw boats out on the water and little houses along the shore. Then at the top of a big hill, Fred said, "Look!" And we see the bay.

We crawled at 20 miles an hour through tiny towns, saw big houses where sea captains and their families lived. Some had tiny rooms on the rooftops, glass on all four sides. "Widows' Walks," Fred said. "It was where a sea captain's wife (and sometimes her children) would go and watch for schooner ships to come home. Looking for the sails to appear on the horizon, way off in the distance. They were called Widows' Walks because not every schooner made it safely back home from its travels. Ships traveled far away, carrying tall, straight tree trunks that would become masts for ships, sailing from Northern Maine lumber camps to Havana, Cuba, where the ships were loaded with goods like coffee beans, which they brought back to Maine. Nowadays, many of these ship captains' homes are bed and breakfast inns for visitors."

We made a meal stop in a historic seacoast schooner town. We ate on a pier: fries and fish burgers (half a fish on a hamburger bun, best fish I ever ate). Here we saw lots of boats: lobster boats, rowboats, canoes, kayaks, and sailing ships of all sizes.

Poem? (Maybe yes. Maybe no.)

Back in van and truck,
Charles kept asking,
"Are we there yet?"
Mom and/or Fred kept answering,
"No, not yet."
We traveled up hills and down.
"A few miles to go," Fred said.
I'm feeling excited.
Then,
"Here's the bridge, built in 1939,"
Fred said.
The Bridge.
Wow.
It went up, up, up, up.
To the highest point:
Our car, 85 feet above the water.

Then
down, down, down, down.
I almost closed my eyes.
Instead, I looked down,
then around.
Mom sighed.
Carrie was asleep.
"We're on Little Deer Isle," Fred said,
whistling.
"Are we there yet?" Charles asked.
"No, not yet," Mom said.
Then . . . a moment later,
"How many feet long
was that bridge?"
Charles asked.
"Total 2,505 feet
across Eggemoggin Reach,"
Fred said. "Look,
here's The Causeway."
The Causeway is almost
as scary as the bridge.
It's a narrow road
with big boulders along the edges
to keep cars or trucks from going off.
Water laps on one side,
mud mucks on the other.
"Low tide," Fred said.
"Ew!" we said.
ANOTHER long hill.
Fred put left blinker on,
and turned where a sign said:
Private Lane.

(End of rough draft for a poem?)

5:00 p.m. Fred parked the van beside a log cabin house.

"Here?" Charles and I asked.

"Here," said Fred.

"Big," Charles said.

"Should be big enough: five bedrooms and four baths," Mom said.

Two minutes later, Pat parked between our van and a smaller log cabin cottage.

"Two bedrooms, two baths," Mom said. "This is where Mrs. Sullivan, Pat, and Toni will stay."

"We're here!" Fred and Pat shouted at the same time.

Everyone except Carrie clambered out fast as possible. We stretched our arms up into the dark blue sky. We looked side to side and saw white birches, oaks, and big tall evergreens. We looked in front of the house and cottage: there was a blueberry field (or "barren," as they're called here). We looked beyond and saw the Bay. It was very dark blue. We sucked in clean, fresh air. It was so clean and clear it almost hurt to breathe.

"Cleansing lungs time: let out all the old air," Mrs. Sullivan said.

We did. I felt my belly go concave. Felt my ribs touch my spine.

"Now breathe in through your nose. Breathe in as much as you can. Hold it. Then out through your mouth," Mrs. Sullivan demonstrated. "Repeat six times."

We did.

"Good. Don't forget to repeat good breathing out, in, out, in, whenever you can. Here is where you'll get rid of all that bad stuff; here you'll heal your body with all this good fresh air."

"Time for everyone to pitch in and unload these packed vehicles," said Fred.

"Oh no."

"Can't it wait?"

Everyone wanted to explore everything all at once: outside everywhere, inside investigate the house and cottage.

"No, not yet," Fred said.

Mrs. Sullivan helped Mom take a sweaty, sleepy Carrie out of the car seat.

Fred and Pat went to find the keys to the house and cottage. They're owned by the same man, and he had told Fred and Pat where they're hidden.

The rest of us started hauling our stuff . . . . AND other stuff out of the van and truck.

"After you have gotten all of your belongings, pick your rooms, unpack, and then you're free to explore. Dinner will be late," Mom said. "Mrs. Sullivan and I need to find a local store, stock up for a few meals. No way are we shopping two weeks' worth of groceries when we're hungry and tired. We want to have fun time, too!".

Finished. Everything unloaded. Ralph and T. L. Toni head hand in hand to the beach.

Charles and I watched for about 3 megaseconds, which was enough time to know we would go in another direction. No way were we going anywhere near where they'd be scooting off to.

We grabbed our backpacks, pillows, and canvas bags filled with our stuff. Charles and I like to travel light.

We "two-stepped" at one time the four steps to the deck of the wraparound porch.

Then we saw something strange. The back door was open.

There was a screen door.

Charles put his forehead against the screen "to see better."

It moved.

The doors weren't locked.

We were scared at first, but it didn't feel "Scary."

This was the moment I got it!

What signs said at different stops we'd made after crossing the bridge out of New Hampshire and into Maine. *Maine, the Way Life Should Be.* Maine, the place where people left doors unlocked AND it was okay.

Charles and I pushed open the screen door and went into a big living room. It has a high, high cathedral ceiling and on a beam there's a ceiling fan. On one side is a bright red wood-burning stove; on the other side, a dining room; around a wall is a galley kitchen.

Sniff. Sniff! Something smelled sweet. We followed our noses. There on the dining room table was a blueberry pie. I touched. It was still warm. Beside it, a note from the owner's wife read: "Enjoy!"

I thought, *this is a good sign.*

"Wait," said Charles. "Turn the note card over. Does it say anything else?"

I did and it did.

It said:

> "It will happen at some time
>
>   Be it while the sun is bright
>
> Or on a starry night."

"What does that mean?" Charles asked.

"How should I know? I just read what it said. It might not even be a note to us. The baker of the pie may be recycling."

"But what IF the note IS to us? Is it a warning? Is something bad going to happen? Or something good?" Charles asked.

"I guess we'll find out. . . ." I said.

End of Journal entry for August 11, 1985

Chapter 1
3:30 a.m. The Day Begins

ha' time is it?" a sleepy Max asked. He pulled the sheets and comforter over his head.

"3:30."

"Way too early, Charles. Go back to sleep. Wake me when it's *really* morning. Not the middle of the night."

"But it is morning *here*, Max," Charles said, full of restless energy. "Remember where we are? Deer Isle, Maine. Lobster boats are roaring away from the docks. Listen, you can hear them—3:30 and they're off beginning their day: check traps, see what's in them. Remove lobster, measure, store the right-sized ones, put others back into the bay. Crabs in the traps? Measure them. If big enough, keep them in separate wet box containers. Throw others back into the bay to swim away. Remove old bait bags, replace with fresh, filled with herring 'delights.' Rotten stuff from stinky bait bags is yummy food for seagulls. As each trap is ready, drop it back into the water. Traps sit on the bottom tied to lines called pot warps. Two or more pots, one warp float over; above on the bay surface bounces a buoy. Each buoy is painted in the lobster person's colors and patterns. A buoy is on display on each lobster boat. Everyone knows which lobster person has which lobster spot. Then it's time to shove the boat in gear and motor to the next spot. Lots of work and dangerous when there are many traps, many ropes, and when people move too quickly and with too little sleep. Think how early those guys must get out of their sacks in order to motor off to sea by 3:30!"

"Well, I guess I better cross being a lobsterman off my career list. Hey, how'd you get to know all those lobster facts?" Max moaned.

"Read it in literature I picked up at the Visitors' Center: *The REAL Romantic Life of Being a Lobster Catcher*. Good reading. I'll lend it to you." Charles pushed sheets and comforter off. "Anyway, it's OUR Birthday. We have to make a real day out of it. Happy B' Day, big bro! Finally, twelve. You made it."

"Happy birthday, right back at you, Charles. You made it to nine and you're still alive!" Max yawned. He wanted to sleep, find a dream, any dream, get a few extra winks before starting his birthday, but inside he knew no way *that* would ever happen.

"Okay, Charles, you win." Max rolled out of bed, found his jeans, pulled them up. Searched around on the floor and found more clothes; pulled on a hoodie sweat shirt. Brr! It was colder than their home in Maryland. He yanked on wool socks Mom had insisted he bring. "Aw, cozy." Then put on his hiking shoes. "So, Mr. Nine-Year-Old, what's the plan?" Max asked.

"Find out what morning here really is like. Maybe, since it's chilly, take our comforters with us. I want to check out the porch swing. I also want to see which birds are the first noisemakers: crows or seagulls?"

"Is that it? Man, you could do all of that from right here looking out the open window. Charles, it's not even sunrise yet." Max was ready to go back to bed.

"Right, sunrise is 5:34. I checked the charts last night."

"5:34! Charles, that's two hours from now. I'm going back to bed." Max reached to untie the laces of his hiking shoes.

16

"Actually, what I really want to do is go down to the beach and see what's happening there. I mean, how often do we have a beach in our front yard?"

"But, Charles, it's so dark we might not find the path to the beach. We might get lost." Max had one shoe lace untied and was working on the other.

"Come on, you're already dressed and not even yawning. We can eat breakfast; eat whatever we want, because it's our birthday. Mom stocked up lots of choices. Then we can grab a snack, go on the porch, check out crows vs. gull wars as it begins to get light. I've been reading up on it: there are big discussions between crow and gull watchers over personalities, bodies, sizes, and attitudes of crows and gulls. Not a lovey-friendly relationship between those two flyers; feuds fester frequently into feathery fights."

Max applauded Charles on his alliteration and debate deliverance (Charles had joined the school debate team last spring semester; a beginner, he was making great progress.). "Okay. Okay, yeah, that makes more sense. We'll have a good meal, pack something to snack on later, grab a couple of water bottles, and meander down for sunrise on the sands." Max retied the lace and grabbed his empty backpack.

When they had arrived the evening before, both boys emptied their backpacks onto the floor and pushed all of their clothes into four of the huge dresser's drawers: two for Max, two for Charles. Now, with their clothes all a jumble inside closed drawers, the boys felt right at home.

Tiptoeing from their room, they were glad their mom assigned rooms for them on the first floor near the library: a multipurpose room with a tiny TV which got two snowy stations, and the sound was like a scratchy 45 record from when their parents were little. The room was also filled with bookshelves: built-in, floor-to-ceiling, and under all the windows, with stacks of books sorted and marked using the Dewey Decimal System. And in a free-standing bookcase, they had found many board games and puzzles. Scattered around the room beside comfy chairs, lamps were placed for cozy reading. And there were other tables with stools for games and puzzles. A 5000-piece puzzle of shells on a beach had been started, as had a chess game with pieces in tense combat position. Across from the library was a full-size bathroom with big shower and tub. (Mom and Fred had their own master suite with Jacuzzi tub and full bath, plus a small room for Carrie). Down the hall was Ralph's bedroom. And, at the very end, double-panel sliding doors opened into a winterized screened-in porch looking into the woods. Upstairs were more bedrooms. One of them their mom was using as her writing studio; beside it was another bathroom.

It was a roomy house with hardwood floors and thick carpets in places where footsteps might wake people sleeping in or taking naps.

The living room rug pictured a fir forest and small cabin with smoke coming from its chimney. It was a thick, warm, wool rug perfect for sitting or lying on while story-telling, reading, drawing, or listening in front of the dark red woodstove. A perfect gathering place ready and waiting, no matter if it were night or day.

In the kitchen, the boys made themselves a breakfast of fruit juice, bowls of cereal, and muffins juicy with newly harvested Maine blueberries from the bakery down the street. Their mom and Mrs. Sullivan had filled bags at the bakery with loaves of different breads: oatmeal, blueberry, eight-grain, cinnamon swirl. Max took a knife and cut two big hunks of oatmeal bread. He found a package of sandwich

18

bags, took two, wrapped the bread in paper towels, then placed each in its own paper bag: one for Charles and one for him. Both boys stuffed their backpacks by adding bananas and bottled water. They were set.

It was 4:45 a.m. when they stepped out onto the porch and into the quiet.

The loudest sound was the squeak of the porch swing as they climbed on and wrapped up in their comforters to keep out the cold damp of morning. An eyelash moon was setting. It was dark, but moment by moment it became more of a creamy gray. Cozy in comforters, rocking ever so slightly in the porch swing, both boys dozed. Time passed, then. . . .

The cawing began.

Not one seagull was in sight.

"Awakened by caws," Max said with a yawn.

"That answers my question about who arrives first: crows or seagulls," Charles said.

Moments went by. "Those are the biggest crows I've ever seen," said Charles.

Two more crows arrived. As time went by, there were no more new black-feathered arrivals, only four in all. Perhaps two couples. Very different crow behavior from what they'd watched at their grandparents' home in Maryland, where crows arrived in a flock (or murder).

The Deer Isle crows chose branches on shade trees beside the house and cottage. They were twice the size of any crow the boys had ever seen. Their feathers were deep black and looked as if they'd been dyed blue, then rubbed shiny with wax.

"They must be ravens," Max said.

"Yep, I think so," said Charles. "I read on the trip here: Ravens have thick necks, shaggy throat feathers, knifelike beaks, and are antisocial. They tend to come in pairs. When they walk, they hop two-footed hops."

"Well, so far they're in pairs on tree branches. No one is hopping on the drive or anywhere else."

"Well, we haven't spread any cracked corn or goodies like bread crumbs for them. I think they're checking us out. If we want them to come nearer, we need to provide goodies. Max, maybe you better mark your journal with a starred note: For future crow encounters, feed them to earn their confidence."

Max and Charles continued to watch.

The crows cackled to each other, bobbed heads, stretched wings, and observed the two whispering human mounds who were trying to stay still on the old porch swing, as if they'd been turned into statues.

Then, in the distance, came a high-pitched call. It was definitely not a caw. Circling high they arrived: a flock of black-backed seagulls, showing off their white heads, necks, and underparts in the shining first light. Several landed on the roof of the cottage, settling wings, showing off pink legs and yellow bills. They were quite handsome. As soon as they'd settled, a staring contest began: gull eyes aimed at the four crows.

Then more gulls came.

"Here come the gulls!" Charles sang to the tune of an "oldie" he'd learned from Mom and Fred (one they'd learned as teens). He wasn't sure what the real words were so he made up his own describing the gulls. "Some are flashing, some are dashing, all are crashing on this crow morning. Here come the gulls."

Crow feet moved up and down on the branches, eyes signaled messages to each other. It was obvious the crows would rather not be seen in the company of seagulls. "Time to go" seemed to be the consensus as more gulls began to land on the cottage's roof.

A few minutes went by: two, three, four. The crows twisted, heads bobbed, they checked in with each other, then decided to fly.

"Score one for the seagulls!" Max said.

"Come on," hissed Charles. "The day is zipping fast."

Max shook his head, and thought: *Up at 3:30. Ready to explore by 4:00. Now, on the move again, a fast-timed track. Charles, you're really trying to make each minute of our birthday special; not a second to be slouched away. Twelve and nine. I wonder what else today or tonight we'll be gifted with?*

Chapter 2
Sunrise on the Shore and Someone More?

"I t's 5:05. Sunrise is 5:34; don't you think we should head down to the shore?" Charles asked.

"Sure."

They took the sandy, twisty path between two blueberry fields. The berries had already been harvested.

"Blueberry harvesting season almost always begins on August 1," Charles told Max.

"And you read this information in one of the free info brochures you picked up yesterday?"

"Of course."

"How many brochures did you take from there?" Max sighed. *It's great having Charles eager to learn, but sometimes I wish he'd cartoon more,* he thought. *Oh, erase that. Restart. Be content Charles is a good informational guide.*

"Twenty."

"Twenty!"

"Yes, but some were general information on farming, harvesting, environmental issues. I found lots about Deer Isle: history, things to do, must-see places, wars fought, domestic arguments. Fun stuff like that."

"I'm sure you won't let us miss a thing while we're here," said Max. *Charles is emerging from the fog: will he be a teacher, professor, or go into marketing?* he thought.

Even though the blueberry fields had been harvested, the boys found plenty of berries along the way to snack on.

"Yum, small and full of flavor," Max said.

Charles gave him a thumbs-up.

They stopped talking, walked in silence, listened: their footsteps crunched the sand, leaves on birch trees rattled while the maple and oak trees lazily stirred as easterly breezes shifted through them. In the distance, but ever closer, sounds of bay surf waves rolled onto the shore. On another day, in another place or time, the boys may have raced: "Who could arrive at water's edge first, find *the* best rock and claim it as his throne: King for the Sunrise." On this day, however, they were content to watch the ever-growing whiter-whiter morning and not tempted to challenge each other. They kept secret what they were feeling, but each felt embraced and almost carried forward by the dawning day.

The path ended where a hedge of blooming beach roses had been cut to create an entrance to the beach. Mixed with morning, salty sea, the sweet rose fragrance was forceful and they felt almost as if they were falling deeper and deeper into a dream. Max and Charles stopped walking, closed their eyes, and breathed cleansing breaths, as Mrs. Sullivan had showed them the evening before.

"Out with the old," Max whispered.

"In with the new," whispered Charles.

"Out with all the bad," Max whispered.

"In with all the good," whispered Charles.

They opened their eyes and slapped high-fives.

"To the beach and sunrise," said Max in a quiet voice. He stepped forward and began looking for a choice rock to sit on.

In the miles of open beach space, they had room to separate and do their own thing, find their own boulder, climb it, claim it as their own; be the Sunrise King of one big stone on this beautiful morning. *I bet the Sunrise King or Sunrise Queen is not written about in any fancy free brochure,* Max thought, as he looked for his perfect throne.

But plans change at any time and any age, even when it is your birthday and when you are nine or twelve years of age. And so it was with this first sunrise on Deer Isle.

Max saw her first.

She was sitting on a huge boulder, face turned not completely toward the sea, and she was definitely not looking in his direction. Her long, red-brown hair swirled the way the tides were swirling around several small beach boulders. She made no effort to keep her hair from covering her eyes or flying near her mouth, and yet, as if she shouted a command, long strands strayed over her brow, under her chin, around her shoulders but away from her eyes and her mouth. Her hands were anchored on the boulder; she stretched long legs that seemed attached to the rock but below her knees, red rubber boots with big feet were tapping to the sound of the surf's hushing. Her head was lifted slightly up. Except for the tapping of those bright red rubber boots and her whirling hair, she could have been a sculpture.

Max stopped and stared.

Charles continued walking in the opposite direction looking for the best boulder.

He never noticed the girl. Within moments, he'd found his choice for a throne. He scrambled up, sat, wiggled until he'd found the hollowed place that fit him best. Only then did he start looking for Max and only then did he see the girl. But Charles, who now was nine, saw some girl on a huge stone. He wondered: *Who is that? How'd she get here? What's her story?* Then he shelved all those potential questions for later and concentrated on why he was on the beach at 5:35 (he checked his watch). He rested back on top of *his* special spot and stared at the sky as it began to color.

Not so Max.

Max saw not just a girl but someone he wanted to meet, maybe, or flee from. He was, if not frozen in his tracks, at least his actions forward were on "pause." *Maybe she doesn't see me here,* he decided.

As quietly as he could, he looked for a place to sit. He chose a long flat ledge, and when he lay on his back, he almost blended in with the rocky gray. *Perfect,* he thought. He arranged his backpack into a pillow, careful not to mush bread or bananas, and rested still as . . . well, yeah, except for breathing, heart booming, pulse tapping, blood roaming, stomach gurgling, he was as still as stone. He stared up and around. The sky was an enormous white canvas slowly beginning to color. But unlike Charles, who was transfixed by the sun rising into the sky, Max was distracted by the girl. Often his eyes, though not his head, looked in her direction.

Besides the long red-brown hair and big red rubber fishing boots, he saw that she wore bibbed blue jean overalls, and over her shirt, hanging down nearly to her knees, a chocolate-brown sweater, sleeves rolled up so her hands were not hidden. Yet even in baggy clothes, Max could tell she was thin and probably very muscular. And, yes, oh gee, she was pretty in an outdoor-loving, tomboyish way.

It was not a "red sky at morning sailors take warning" sunrise. Instead, a gold sky glowed as the sun appeared to rise from up the bay. Yellows streaked skyward as the sun went higher into the nearly cloudless sky: golden colors changing into pale blue, to blue-blue, many shades of blue.

"No storm today. No storm tonight. Very okay, wouldn't you say?" The girl was speaking to Max.

"Well, yes. Great! Ah, perfect," Max said. He awkwardly pushed away from the flat ledge. He'd been schooled that a gentleman always rose to greet someone.

But before Max could walk to her rock, the girl had slid down and was headed over to him with her right hand outstretched. When she was about two feet away, she stopped. The sleeve of her baggy sweater had rolled down and was covering over her "handshake hand." She pushed it back to her shoulder, but it slid back to her wrist. Before it could slip further, she took another step and, honoring the "18 inch I'm American we don't get into your personal space rule," greeted him.

"I'm Zipper, short for Zipporah, from the Tiberian vocabulary meaning *bird*. Chirp-chirp! My parents liked names one never hears, names not in the mainstream. Zipporah was the wife of Moses. You could say she was someone who knew all about the wilderness experience. Anyway, great to share this good news Monday morning sunrise with . . . ?"

"Zipporah, Zipper. Wow. Oh, yeah, I'm Max," he said taking her hand and giving her a firm but not hurtful handshake. He noticed her palms were tough. *Must do hard work,* he thought.

She gave him a firm handshake back.

Hmm, he thought, then said, "Um, let's see, my name, Maximus, from the Latin *greatest*. What were my parents thinking!? Oh, yeah. There was this Saint Maximus who lived in the seventh century. He was a monk and theologian in Constantinople."

"Today on the beach at sunrise a bird girl meets a monk boy." She gave his hand another shake. "Pretty cool."

"And over there, on the biggest boulder he could find, is my little brother, Charles. He's okay. Actually, he's really smart. Ah, his name was originally from the German and then the French. Roughly, it translates as *free man*. Well, he's not a man yet, but today *is* his birthday. Today he's nine."

26

"Really? My birthday was on August 7. I turned twelve."

"REALLY! Actually, Charles and I share a birthday . . . my birthday is today, too. I'm twelve today," he said.

"I'm five days older than you but we're both twelve and we're both Leos."

"Yep," Max said. He was up on this one; he loved horoscope stuff. "And Leos get along okay with other Leos."

They finally stopped shaking hands. Zipper pushed her sleeve up and held it with her other hand.

Max shoved both hands into his hoodie's front pouch.

"Hey, have a rock," she said, offering him a rock where two boulders were about two feet high and three feet apart.

"Okay."

"Yep, Leo's a good sign. I like being a Leo," Zipper said. "It's great to meet others. To meet other people no matter what their horoscope sign is. Where are you from?"

"I was about to ask you," Max said. "I'm from, as they say up here, from away. We just arrived here yesterday. We're here for two weeks. My first time, Charles's first time to Maine. It's great. And you?"

"I'm from away too. I don't live on Deer Isle. I live on an island off of Stonington. Isle au Haut, ever heard of it?"

"Yep, saw it on a map. That's cool. Always lived there?"

"A long time, but no, I was born in Massachusetts. That makes me really from away. My parents moved here when I was five. I'm the oldest of two. Like you, except, we're both girls. My sister's name is Perri, short for periwinkle. I think my parents were thinking of the little blue flowers. We moved here when she was two. I never thought much about her name until one of the islanders took me to see periwinkle snails. When I came home and told my parents they said, 'Well, periwinkle snails are pretty cool. Check them out in the tidal pools when the tide is out.' So I did. And I decided they're great snails. I've never made fun or let anyone else make fun of Perri's name, or for that matter, I don't let other kids bully or make someone feel different for stupid reasons like 'Oh, you don't understand. You're from away!' Anyway, another day, another story. Perri will be nine in September. She's Libra. We get along like Tony the Tiger says," she paused and looked at Max. "She's . . . ."

Max got the cue and with her he repeated the old commercial slogan:

"Grrrrrrrrrrrrrrrreat!"

"Grrrrrrrrrrrrrrrreat!"

They laughed. Max didn't know about Zipper, but he was feeling pretty great inside. Here he was way up in Maine on vacation and he'd met someone his age who seemed to be like him. She didn't act sissified. She was a girl who liked nature.

"What are you doing all the way here from Isle au Haut so early this morning?" Max asked. Then he felt embarrassed. *Here I've just met her and I'm asking her a personal question.* Aloud he said, "I'm sorry, none of my business."

"Huh?" Zipper looked at him, puzzled. "Not personal at all. My dad dropped me off. He was headed over to the pier in Blue Hill. I wanted to see sunrise here. "

"But, uh, why here? I mean it's really pretty and everything, but . . . ."

"It's very pretty. It's a great beach for watching sunrise and sunsets on, and usually nobody's around. Not much boat action. My dad dropped me here, yes, to see the sunrise, but afterwards to go to the cottages. My Uncle Pat, he and his wife Popee, are supposed to have arrived last night with

28

friends. Over there," Zipper said pointing to the cottage and house across the blueberry field.

"No way!" said Max.

"Yes, way!" Zipper said. She frowned. "Why?"

"Because we're the friends. Pat and Mrs. Sull . . . I mean, Popee, are staying next to us. They're chaperoning my brother Ralph's girlfriend. . . ."

"Toni?"

"Yeah. My stepdad is Fred. He and Pat are best friends. Our mom is best friends with Mrs. Sul . . . I mean, Popee. Oh, I give in. Charles and I call Popee Mrs. Sullivan . . . I know it's crazy because we call Pat, Pat, but we know Popee as a teacher and we are *so* into calling all teachers like we do in school. Anyway, she says she's used to it. She's way cool."

"No worries, I understand. Dad never told me Uncle Pat was coming with another family who had people close to my age."

Her smile made Max smile. He bet everyone smiled when they saw Zipper's smile and her sparkling dark eyes, the darkest brown eyes he'd ever seen. They were like the earth at its darkest.

About then, Charles rock-hopped over and all the introductions and explanations began all over again.

Finally, they arrived at a pause place. By now they were sitting on rocks close to each other but all facing the bay.

"Oh, hey, I'm being rude. Are you hungry, Zipper? Charles and I have bakery bread and bananas we can share."

"No sweat. My pack is loaded with apples, bread, and a jar filled with water to drink. We can share."

Which is what they did.

Chapter 3
Tidal Pools and Crab Racing, Really?

U sing a large rock ledge as a table and sitting cross-legged, Zipper, Max, and Charles shared food from their packs. It was a simple feast of fresh bakery breads, blueberries Zipper had picked at the beginning of August, apples, bananas, bottles of water (and in Zipper's case, a large jar of water with lemon wedges in it). For dessert, Zipper cut slices of fresh brown sugar fudge her mother had made. Over their heads, the sunrise colors changed into darker and darker blues; the bay, too, became darker. Beyond them seagulls were gathering. One or two seemed to call for a mate, friend, child, by making loud shrieking noises. Other gulls were murmuring in "conversation" with each other. Two or three gulls found boulders away from the group. Others rested on the bay, drifting with the tide.

"The gulls like it out there. Their behavior will change soon when the tide recedes and the mud flats between them and where we are sitting become a 'grocery store,' then you'll see how they really are. Some gulls have better dining manners than others. Some have no manners at all."

"Like some middle school kids I know," Charles said. "Present company excluded, of course." He poked Max.

Max ignored him. He turned the topic back to crows and gulls and what he and Charles had seen earlier that morning: crows arriving first in what looked like two couples and how they reacted to the gulls. "As if the seagulls were invading their privacy."

"Every morning," said Zipper, shaking her head like a mother might when describing an impolite child. "You'd think they'd get tired of playing those same old games, but they don't."

"Maine crows are different from crows we have at home. They look different, too," Charles said.

"That's because the crows you saw this morning were ravens. They have a totally different personality," Zipper said. "They're real loners, mate for life, are rather antisocial, and they're much bigger than regular crows."

"Yep, I read about them in a brochure I picked up at the Maine Visitors' Center," Charles said.

"A visitors' center? I've never been there."

"Really?" Max and Charles said at once.

"No, I hardly get too far off island. I mean, the island where I live, Isle au Haut. Occasionally, trips to visit family, but you know . . . anyway, when you live here, you really don't need to go to some visitors' center to see what Maine is like."

"Yes, I understand," said Max. "It's that way in Maryland where we live." He turned to Charles. "How many times did we ever stop at the Maryland visitors' centers?"

"Never. I mean, we have them? Where?" Charles asked.

"Route 95 North. One is called The Maryland House. Very cool, we stopped there on a school trip once. We were on a trip to some museum near the Maryland–Delaware line," Max said.

The day was warming. The two boys pulled off their hooded sweat shirts and Zipper shrugged off her great wool sweater. Max wore a T-shirt from his school: it was pale blue and on the left side was an emblem with a bird and the school's name, *Blue Bird*, sewn on with darker blue threads. Charles wore a white shirt with green trim around the neck. It was one of his old, worn swim team uniform shirts. Stamped on in green ink was a drawing of a swimmer's head and five lines to represent water waves; on the back his team number: 7. Zipper's bibbed overalls hid part of her shirt, but what was visible was waffle-weave long underwear in a creamy yellow color. Max thought, *Strange a yellow, long underwear shirt could actually look nice on someone.* He caught himself before saying, "Great shirt."

"Hey, you guys, great shirts, too," Zipper said. "Charles, what's with the number? Is that a swimmer?"

"Uh?" Charles pulled his shirt out so he could see what he was wearing. He'd picked this shirt because it was on top of the messy pile. "I belong to a swim team and my number is 7."

"You compete in swim matches? You swim in pools? Clubs?"

"Well, in the summer I swim at the swimming club our family belongs to. It's really close by. Yes, I swim in meets. I swim the crawl most the time, but I'm getting better and better at the butterfly. Someday I hope to swim the butterfly in meets, but only when I'm much better and faster at it."

"You swim in pools and you swim all year?" Zipper asked.

"Yeah, we have a pool at school. Sometimes during the school year, meets are held at our school or other schools with pools. Special meets are held at a big fancy indoor pool where Olympic swimmers train. But I've only gone there a few times for district meets."

"Most of the kids down your way are given swimming lessons?"

"A lot, but not all," said Max. "I've taken swim lessons, too, but I only swim for fun. I really don't like swimming in pools. Chlorine burns my eyes and nose when they don't have it mixed right. Do you swim?"

"Well, yes, I do, but the only times I've ever been swimming in manmade pools is when my family goes on vacation, when we stay in a hotel or visit someone with one. There are no swimming clubs on the island where I live, none on Deer Isle or any nearby. Very few kids or adult fisherfolk have ever had any swimming lessons."

"Really!" Max and Charles exclaimed.

"Yeah. It's pretty sad. We have some great places to swim or at least to wade in. We have some ponds . . . . One close by is my favorite and then, when you cross the bridge, there are lakes. Some summer camps, fancy ones and church ones, located on big ponds. Kids go there. There are many places over on MDI, um, Mount Desert Island, where Bar Harbor is, but it's a long trip from here. The pond on Deer Isle is best! Every summer, one of the church leaders gets her granddaughter who's a professional lifeguard to give swim lessons there."

"How about the bay?" Max asked, looking out at the receding tide.

"Sure. But it's really cold unless you swim in certain coves. When it's been a hot day and the bay is going out over hot sand and stones, then it's decent."

"I hope we have a chance to explore all the swimming places," Charles said.

"Oh, I'm sure Uncle Pat and Fred will take you. Hey, we should be checking out the tidal pools. Are you both finished eating . . . for now?"

"Sure. Yep, I'm full," said Max.

All three packed up the leftovers, papers, bottles, and put them into their packs. Zipper noticed and approved. "You guys know the rule of pack out what you packed in and leave behind only foot tracks on the sand."

"Of course," said Charles. "Our grandpa is an environmentalist, big time."

"Won an award for it from the State of Maryland before we were born; he started when he was a kid and keeps teaching everybody else," Max said.

"Great," said Zipper. "Hey, look. See how some gulls are diving down?"

"Yea," Max said.

"One just picked up something and is flying into the sky again," Charles added.

"He's got a mussel. Watch what he does," Zipper said.

All eyes were on the gull as it soared carrying a blue mussel in its mouth. They saw him pause in midair, open mouth. They watched as the mussel fell onto a boulder. "Crack!" The gull swooped down, landed almost exactly where the mussel had, worked free the meat, and ate.

"Okay," said Zipper. "That's a gull who knows how it's done," she pointed. "Look. See which one I mean? It has many brown feathers, an immature bird, and they don't always know all the techniques."

As Zipper predicted, the young gull flew to the muddy place, landed, took a few steps, and found a mussel. Like the first gull, it flew into the air with the mussel. It flew up, up, up, then paused and dropped the mussel, which landed not with a crack but a smack onto the mud, not far from another gull. Before the young gull could land and get its mussel, which was still enclosed in shell, and try again, the gull standing on the mud—a craftier seagull—had the mussel in its beak and was flying away.

Zipper pointed. All three watched as the thieving gull flew over a large flat stone ledge and dropped the mussel. They heard a distant sound of breaking shell. The gull swooped down and took its stolen prize.

"Cheater!" Max said.

"No fair," said Charles.

"Welcome to the animal world where all sorts of things happen, especially when experienced gulls see newbies or where rascals look for easy ways to take things they want or need."

"Like some people," Max said.

Zipper looked at him. Their eyes met. They looked away. "Some play unfair games and cheat. When it happens, others get hurt," she said.

There was a moment of quiet as each remembered stories from their own experiences, knowing how some people used or hurt others.

Finally, Zipper said, "The tide is really out now. Let's investigate the tidal pools and see what we can find."

"A challenge? A competition? See who finds what in how long?" Charles asked.

"Well...." said Zipper.

She really doesn't seem to be the competitive type, Max thought. Aloud he said, "Charles, why don't we go and watch." He wanted to see what he could see, learn what he could learn, making no changes, no games.

"Oh, sure," Charles said.

"Follow me," said Zipper. She led them down the beach. They went about ten minutes before she stopped. She pointed to places filled with boulders, rock weed, and tidal pools. "Here's what you do. You squat low. You don't let your shadow cross the pool. You wait quietly. You watch miniature worlds inside the pool."

All three grouped around a big pool left behind when the tide went out. Part of this pool was on top of ledge, part over a sandy, shelly shore. Nearby and far away up and down the beach, they could see other pools gleaming in the sun. Some were surrounded by rocks while others were in muddy places. A large boulder was close to the tidal pool Zipper had picked. It was covered with shabby, slimy gold, brown, dark-green, and almost black weed: *rockweed*.

"Charles, go to the boulder there; lift some rockweed up? It'll be wet but it really isn't too yucky."

"Sure," Charles said. He did what he was told. He bent down and grabbed as much rockweed as he could hold in both hands. He lifted and held it as Zipper instructed him to.

"See anything? Look carefully at the boulder that rockweed was covering."

Max went over to where Charles was. He bent down and looked. He picked up another section of the slime-green overhang. "What's that? Something's in there. Something with parts bigger than my fingers. It's moving slow but it's moving." He reached down and gently pulled. He was able to take it into his hand. "Charles, look! Look what I found," Max said.

As he held the creature, Zipper came closer to see. She smiled a "yes." He'd found what she wanted them to find.

Seeing her smile of "yes," Max felt warm inside.

"What is it?" Charles asked. He looked at the purple, bunched-up creature. Several legs were moving slowly. They were moving as if pulling, then slowly reaching out.

"It's a starfish. Some people call them sea stars, which is a really pretty name, I think. It's moving so it's harder to see

36

the star. We have starfish of all sizes and colors in places near here," Zipper said.

"Really?" asked Max and Charles.

"Really. I know one island, when it's low tide and the mud is thick, great for clamming, you can walk almost the whole way to the island. There's a small channel fishermen have kept open for boats with big keels. On this island, under the rockweed, I've seen orange, yellow, blue, and many purple starfish/sea stars, some bigger than both my hands put together."

"Wow, a starfish that big would really be something to see," Max said.

"Pat brought our rubber raft and some kayaks. Maybe we can go and see them," said Charles.

"Yes, a good trip, but you really have to watch the tides," Zipper said. "If you time your tide wrong, you'll end up walking your raft through some really disgusting mud, scratching your legs on broken mussel shells and other nasty stuff. But if you keep a good watch on the tide, it's a great trip."

"I'm putting this starfish back where I got him," Max said. He put it back by the rock where he had gotten it and pushed rockweed into place.

"Yes, good. Starfish want to be in their own habitat. They also hate the sun and heat; that's why we find them under heavy rockweed, when we have a low tide. Soon the tide will be coming back in again and they'll be happily covered by bay waters."

"Hey," said Charles. He let go of the rock weed he'd been holding. Now he was staring into a different tidal pool. "What's this little snail guy? I think he's moving? Yeah. He's moving . . . going slow. He has a dark brown shell."

"Don't let him see your shadow or he'll stop and try to blend in with the empty shells. There are empty shells all around him, right?" Zipper asked.

"Yep, empty or maybe hiding."

Zipper and Max went to see what Charles had found.

"Charles and I are used to hiding our shadows from water creatures. We live on a farm with ponds and springs where salamanders, frogs, and fish hide," Max told her.

"Good to know you aren't city guys. Good also to know you're not skittish of wild creatures."

Max looked over his brother's shoulder. The tidal pool was filled with periwinkle shells. "It looks like a five-hundred-piece puzzle and I can't see which piece I'm supposed to be looking for. Where is your little guy, Charles?" he asked.

"Next to the big white shell, see? The biggest white shell. The one that looks like two open wings," Charles said.

"An empty scallop shell. Yes, I see it. Something, or more likely someone, took the meat and left the shell," said Zipper. She stood beside Max, looking into the pool. "I see him. It's a periwinkle, a common periwinkle. History says they were eaten in ancient times, but the ones we have in New England are their larger cousins called whelks, which were brought from Western Europe in the 1800s to eat the algae. They do a good job. Whelks and sometimes periwinkles are eaten here, too, though it takes a lot of periwinkles to make a decent appetizer. Boil up and eat. *Bon appétit!*"

"Escargot," said Max. *Those French classes are handy after all,* he thought.

"That's right. Most popular in France and Spain, I've read. But little periwinkles are really cool critters, powerful even though they're small. Oh, I see the one you mean, Charles. Can you see him, Max? He has his tentacles out . . .

he's moving across a rock, which is camouflaged by empty shells of long dead periwinkles." Zipper pointed to a place near the scallop shell.

"Oh, yeah, there he is. Look at him moving his tentacles. They look like they're an important part of his body. Are they?"

"I'll say. They're the way he sees and tastes."

"Whoa! Eyes with taste buds. Cra-zy!" said Charles.

"These little snails, called common periwinkles, *are* amazing. They travel by rippling muscles but can only go forward, I think. I guess we have to watch him to know if he can go backwards. His foot is divided into left and right parts. When he wants to stop and 'close up shop,' he finds a rock or seaweeds, maybe a piling or rocky jetty. Then he goes deep inside his hard shell, excretes sticky mucus stuff; when it dries, it's like glue. He can stay holed up in his shell a long time because he has stored moisture in his gills, safe when it's low tide and he's out of the water, safe in cold weather and hot sunny weather. Quite a guy. He's only about 1 inch by 1 ¾ inch. He's powerful. Periwinkles have radula, which are like tiny teeth. They use them to chew away algae. Years and years later, you can see that they've left trail marks on stones." Zipper told them.

"No way!" said Charles.

"Wind and water erode stone. Now you tell us periwinkles leave trails on stones? Are they like these marks?" Max pointed to one of the large stones. It had long trail marks on it.

"Yes. That's a trail carved by periwinkles." Zipper said.

"I think nature is so rad," said Max.

"Yeah, I agree," added Charles.

"Rad? That means good? *Rad*—is it a new word? I've not heard it before."

"Yep, rad is definitely a plus," Max said.

"Okay, let me show you something special you can do with a periwinkle instead of using them for miniature appetizers. Charles, since you met this little guy first, reach in and take him out of the water," Zipper said.

"Really? Okay." Charles kept his shadow away from the periwinkle's line of vision, picked him up, and carried him out of the water. "Now he's gone in his shell. Do you want him to glue himself to me?"

"Well, it could be interesting," Zipper laughed. "No, he won't if you follow my directions. Place him in the palm of your hand. Put your other palm over him. Make your hands a protective shell. Good. Now, in the place where your thumbs come together and there's a little gap, put your lips right there. Next, I want you to hum. Make up any humming you want but try to make it sound like bay surf when it's calm."

"Okay. I can do that." Charles positioned the periwinkle and his hands as Zipper had instructed. He placed his lips where his thumbs came together and he started humming.

"What's going to happen?" Max asked.

"Shh! Wait. It won't take long. Maybe a minute," Zipper said.

Max and Zipper counted off seconds in their heads.

"Okay, Charles, I want you to stop. Keep your hands like they were when you were humming but open them a wee bit. Look in. What do you see?" Zipper asked.

Charles did as he was told. His face turned from a question mark into a grin.

Zipper motioned Max and they both moved behind Charles's shoulder, looking over it to see.

"You hummed him out," Max whispered.

"Yeah, he has his head out of the shell."

"But not for long. Better put him back where he was," Zipper said.

Charles did as she asked. He wiped his hands on the back of his pants. "That was cool." Charles watched the tidal pool and the little periwinkle he'd just released in it. He felt connected to the little snail. He hoped nothing would hurt it.

"Yeah, it's a wonderful nature trick. Max, you'll have to try it sometime, but right now I have something else to show you guys. Then, well, then we better get ourselves to the cottages because your family is probably awake by now and wondering where you are."

"But please one more trick or something." Charles was almost whining.

"One more for now. Hey, you two have two weeks in Maine *and* are on vacation here. This is only the first morning," Zipper said. "See over here where mud meets tide?"

She led them to a place about four or five feet away from the tidal pool. "There! Do you see anything different about these periwinkle shells?"

The boys looked down where she was pointing. They stared.

Max saw something first. "I see little fins. I see shells moving."

"Me, too," Charles said at last.

"In Maryland, I bet you guys have these crabs, too. Ever hear of hermit crabs?"

"Sure. People buy them in Ocean City, Maryland. O.C. is what we call it. It's a three-hour drive from where we live.

People buy hermit crabs there and in other pet stores closer to our home. Kids keep them as pets," Max said.

"Well, we won't keep these. I don't think it's fair to take something away from its natural environment, but we'll have some fun with them *if* you handle them gently, okay?" Zipper asked.

"We'll be careful," Charles said.

"You can trust us," said Max.

"I know I can. I wouldn't show you this game if I didn't think I could trust you," Zipper said.

Max liked the way she was serious, protected nature, and explained stuff like a good teacher, but best . . . what he noticed when he first met her: he liked her smile. She was always smiling. *And she's only five days older than me,* he thought.

"Okay, I'm going to get a hermit crab for each of us. Be ready for it to try to scoot. Hermit crabs aren't like periwinkles; they're fast and sneaky."

She squatted down, nabbed a shell with little legs poking out and wiggling. When "the giant" moved a hermit crab in its protective shell, immediately all legs tried to hide inside, but the hermit was bigger than the shell it had moved into and his little fins were left sticking out and twitching.

Zipper handed the shell and hermit crab to Max, then found another and snatched it up for Charles. A third she kept for herself. In her other hand she grabbed a handful of empty, bay-wet periwinkle shells. She spread them in a line about six inches from where she was.

"Now kneel down, one of you on each side of me. Think of a horse racetrack. We're going to put down our hermit crabs while they are still in shells and see what happens."

The boys did as Zipper instructed.

Charles looked at Max and said: "On a 1 . . . 2 . . . 3!"

All three placed hermit crab-filled shells down in a line and watched.

Stretch, scramble, skitter, scoot, "skir-winch," each hermit reacted differently as soon as the periwinkle shells were on the ground again and their fins felt the familiar muddy shore. One scuttled in and out of its chosen shell. Two immediately scurried, wiggled zigzagging after new shells. One sprinted from one shell to another inspecting, skipping, scrutinizing, squishing in, too tight, size-up, seize another, squeeze in, strut . . . strut.

Zipper, Max, and Charles laughed at hermit crab antics as these spiderlike critters were speculating, selecting, skittering, shell to shell until, nestling in their chosen "ship shells," they were covered by tidal pool water.

"What fun," Max said.

"Another time, I'll show you how, when I was younger and more people our age lived on Isle au Haut, we'd race green crabs. Or, another favorite game was to see how many empty periwinkle shells we could pile into half a blue mussel shell before it sank. And, of course, we learned how to follow squirting soft shell clams and dig through the mud to get a batch for a meal," Zipper said. "Actually, that's really only the beginning of what island kids do for fun, when we are rock-hopping like kid goats all over the island day after day. But now, Charles, you seem to be the timekeeper; what does your watch say?"

For once, Charles had forgotten time.

Perhaps life is not all about counting, watching seconds tick by on his wristwatch; instead it's about experiencing each moment, Max thought.

Hearing Zipper's request, Charles washed gray muddy hands in a deep tidal pool and reached into the deepest pocket of his jeans for his watch. "Eight o'clock," he said.

"Yep, I was thinking it must be. Okay, we really must go. I'm sure the family is awake and stirring by now and I can't wait any longer to see my Uncle Pat and Aunt Popee." Zipper started walking to the ledge where they'd left their packs.

"We'll be back, all of us, back and exploring some more, right?" Max asked as he stepped quicker to keep pace with Zipper.

"Oh, Max," Zipper turned and looked at him with her dark eyes. "Of course, you will. But there's so much more you'll want to see and do on this day and on this night."

Chapter 4
Plan, Plans, Plans

The trip back to the house and cottage seemed faster than their early morning walk to the shore. It was a bright, shiny morning as Max and Charles returned home with a new friend.

What will happen when we're back with the others? Max thought. *A thrill, chill, nerves on edge, or a terrific birthday filled with surprises? Will it be a birthday that's fun? Or a bummer, bumbling, slow day filled with this and that, ending with cake and candles to blow out? A mix of family and friends? And an awful, off-key singing of "Happy Birthday," which always chokes me up? And maybe I have made a new friend. A real someone who's not a bore, not a snob. And not a guy! A girl and she's not like any girl I've ever met before.*

The last few yards to the cottages became a mad dash to keep pace with Zipper. Then, as soon as she saw her Uncle Pat and Aunt "Popee" (Mrs. Sullivan) standing outside the cottage looking toward the shore, Zipper went full throttle. Soon, she was in Uncle Pat's arms, swinging as Pat whirled her around as if she were on a merry-go-round ride.

"Our Zipper with Max and Charles? Oh my! Zipper, let me look at you. Goodness, you've grown two feet since we were here last!" Aunt Popee said. "Do I get a hug, too?"

"Oh, of course you do!" Zipper held her Uncle Pat's hand as if afraid he might drift away like a helium-filled balloon. She reached for Aunt Popee. "A three-way hug?" Uncle Pat, Aunt Popee, and Zipper did a football-style huddle hug.

"Reunions," said Charles, shrugging his shoulders, "always big tear jerkers."

45

"Don't be smug, Charles," whispered Max. "I can see a bubble of wet in your eyes. I think Zipper reuniting with her uncle and aunt is cool. We get to see them all the time. We know what fun they are . . . even if they're adults."

"Yeah, sorry. I'm being an eight-year-old brat, when I should be glowing the glow, shining the shine of a guy who today turns nine," Charles said. He punched Max's arm in a brotherly way.

"Zip, have you been busy showing these never-been-to-Maine guys why *here* is the best place to be in August?" Pat said.

"They came down during first light, were quiet. They actually soaked in sunrise. So far, I'm impressed by them. They don't have an attitude: 'I'm on vacation here; show me what's so GREAT about Maine. Where's the fast action? What? No carry-out or souvenir pop-up shop on this beach? What gives?' You know, Uncle Pat, how those sorts of summer visitors are and all the stuff they throw at us 'year-rounders' every summer." Zipper lowered her voice to almost a whisper. Her eyes were big, like mirrors reflecting darkness. She shoved her hands deep into the pockets of her overall pants. "You know, some people make me hide and stay away from all the places I love. People with bossy attitudes of: 'I want it all and I want it now' and 'Who are you? You live here? That makes you *not* like me.' Ugh! But not Charles and Max. They seem different. So far, anyway, meeting them makes me feel good. I've had a great morning sharing some of my favorite island secrets with them."

"Perfect!" Pat and Popee said together.

"I had a feeling you three could make a good team." Pat was smiling.

"Tell me," Aunt Popee said. "Have you shown Charles and Max the land of the tidal pools?"

"Yes!" said all three at once. They laughed.

"I held a starfish. Or sea star, as Zipper said they're also called. She showed us where to look to find one," said Max.

"I saw a periwinkle walking over empty shells with his eye-mouth sticking out. When he hid in his shell, Zipper showed me how if I hummed songs that sounded like the tides, he'd come out of his shell and look around. It was wild." Charles said.

"And we saw lots of hermit crabs scrambling in and out of empty shells. We even had a sort of a Preakness Race . . . you know, without horses, gamblers, or bets waged. It was great." Max did two thumbs-up.

"Goodness, I hope you left some things undone and didn't do it all in a few hours," Aunt Popee said to Zipper.

"Oh, no, there are days of things they must do: green crab races, blue mussel weigh-ins, clam digs, rock skips. . . ."

"Excellent," said Pat.

Charles looked at his watch. He looked at Max. He looked at Zipper and the adults. "Are Mom and Fred up? Ralph and T.L.. . . . I mean, Toni, Carrie, and . . . I was just wondering, is there a plan? I mean, special birthday type of stuff for Max and me and . . . well, just wondering?"

"Charles, the Keeper of the Minutes. I love it," said Pat. He laughed at his own joke. "Of course there's a plan."

"Breakfast was first, but judging from what your mom and I saw when we went to make it, two rather large mice, or rats, must have beaten us to it," Popee said. She laughed. "So we can move on to step two."

"Which is to discuss who wants to do what next and with whom," said Pat. "There are options. It is a beautiful day. My idea is *not* staying inside."

Everyone agreed with Pat.

"Never on a day like today," Max said.

Just then Fred came outside. Mom was right behind him carrying baby Carrie. A moment later, stretching, sighing, scratching his long shaggy hair, Ralph stepped onto the deck. The bright sun blinded him for a moment. He put his left hand across his forehead like a sunshield on a cap. Unlike the other men, and definitely unlike the boys, Ralph was dressed in stone-washed, tight jeans, a black T-shirt from a Queen concert he'd attended. Over it, he wore an unbuttoned, collared dress shirt, sleeves rolled at his elbows. He looked like a fashion model one would see in a Lands' End catalog mixed with someone featured in *Rolling Stone Magazine*.

Last to leave the house was Toni. She was dressed (costumed) in her "Valley Girl Goes to Maine" outfit straight out of a "Summer, 1985 L.L. Bean Catalog": stone-washed tight jeans, pink polo shirt, and matching pink "jellies" on her feet.

Max looked at Zipper and rolled his eyes. She winked back. Charles decided it was a good moment to turn his back, look down, pretend the sun was in his eyes, and check his watch. Introductions were quickly made, then Pat returned to a plan for the day.

"We have many options and two vehicles. The walk to the shore is short, as is the walk to the bakery, or trails through the woods. We have one blow-up rubber raft with a battery-powered pump making it ready to float in about ten minutes, and you won't end up breathless. We have two kayaks, little and beamy, fun to ride. Not as fast as sea kayaks

48

but good for adventures and island-hopping tours. If we need sea kayaks, I bet Zipper knows who to contact."

"Sure do."

"As for shopping. . . ." Aunt Popee jumped in.

Before T.L. Toni zones out from boredom on Day 1 in Maine, Max thought.

"As for shopping," Aunt Popee repeated. She had gotten Toni's attention. "In Deer Isle village, there's The Periwinkle Shop, good for locally written books, candles, table decorations, puppets, island-made wooden toys. It really is a must-see. It has been ever since it opened in 1966. We can also take Route 15 to Burnt Cove, where there are a couple of stores. One shop sells everything from furniture, lamps, chinaware to clothes, shoes and hats, fishing gear, swimming musts, souvenir photos, and snacks. Besides, it is actually attached to a decent grocery store. Amazing stores. Driving further we will arrive in Stonington, which is located at the very tip of the island. There are quite a few shops there, art galleries, and good places to snack."

A look of interest flickered across Toni's face.

Mrs. Sullivan (but now I'll always think of her as Zipper's Aunt Popee) sure knows how to read a mood and what to do, what to say, how to save the moment, Max thought.

"Or there's a beautiful trail, not a hard one, not a long one; if you fast-pace, it'll take an hour. If you go slow, one and a half or two hours or more. It's through a good mix of woods, bay, caves, and a pink granite pebble beach. If you know which blue trail marker to take, there's even a family graveyard. Rather haunting. If you're into reading messages on graves, take some paper and crayons so you can do rubbings. Rubbings will allow you to usually read what weather-worn messages were written. If you choose this trip, the next stop would be a snack at a local store, then a swim at The Lily Pond," Pat said.

"I happen to know a couple of people here who once had an interesting experience with old gravestones," said Fred, glancing over at Charles and Max.

"Yeah, it was cool. We never did a rubbing, though, didn't need to. I like those plans, Fred. Being able to read some eroding messages . . . . Well, it just sounds pretty cool," said Max.

"Let me see if I have Pat's plan in order," said Charles. "Hike where the graveyard is, grab something to eat, go for a swim?"

"Yep. Swim in The Lily Pond where we could easily take the kayaks or the raft," Pat said.

"Uncle Pat, don't forget The Lily Pond has a place for sunbathing, a place for babies to play in shallow water, other places where people go fishing. And," Zipper paused and looked at Ralph, "there's a trail to a Tarzan swing only used by older teens, people older and braver than I'll ever be. Well, maybe when I'm sixteen or seventeen or eighteen. It's really scary. It is *the* place where the older kids go."

"Oh, yeah? What makes it scary?" Ralph challenged her. Suddenly his interest was tweaked.

"Well, I've never done it, but I've seen island guys do it. You have to climb high up this rickety ladder built on the side of a big rock ledge, then take the rope swing and lunge forward as hard as you can. You swing out as far as you can go, where the water of the pond is the deepest: 26 feet deep. When you've swung out as far as you can, you let go. It's about a 25- to 30-foot drop. If you aren't out far enough, you can cut your legs on sharp rocky ledges," Zipper said.

"If true, The Lily Pond to kayak and maybe the rope swing is my choice." Ralph said.

"It's true. Every word Zip said. Actually I've done it. It's something you never forget," Pat said.

"Okay, well, take a bit of time . . . like ten minutes or so, then let Fred, Pat, Mrs. Sullivan (Aunt Popee) know. We'll get ready for this most amazing day," Mom said.

Max, Charles, and Zipper knew exactly what they wanted to do and shopping was *not* it.

After some discussion it was decided. Max, Charles, and Zipper would go with Fred and Pat to hike, snack, then to The Lily Pond for swimming and kayaking. Ralph, Toni, Mom, Carrie, and Aunt Popee would go shopping, meet the others for a snack of ice cream, and then they'd go to The Lily Pond, too.

"Okay," said Mom. "Take about 30 minutes. Change into bathing suits under your clothes; you need to get bath towels and sensible shoes if you're hiking; bug dope, sunscreen, extra water bottles in portable coolers. I'll buy and bring other snacks, light lunch stuff. We'll all work together to haul everything we want for lunch, swimming, boating down the path to The Lily Pond."

"It's a good plan," said Pat. "I think everybody will have a chance to do something they like. Zipper, your family knows you're spending the day, evening, night with us, right?"

"Yes, thanks, Uncle Pat. Dad brought me over to the beach this morning. I have changes of clothes with me. I even brought a swimsuit and something to dress in later."

"Good!" Mom said. "Because in the late afternoon, we'll return here, clean up, and go out to dinner. Then we'll be back for something very special."

Something special after dark, hmm, I wonder? Max thought.

Chapter 5
Hiking in Paradise

Part 1:

On The Way to The Park Through Paradise

P opee and Mom had found materials for stone rubbings. Popee stuffed a roll of paper and box of 100 crayons into Fred's pack.

All dressed for an outside adventure day and all packed in less than 30 minutes, Pat, Fred, Zipper, Max, and Charles climbed into Pat's truck and drove off to hike the trail. They left the others in various stages of clothes changing, preparing, and packing.

Max, Charles, and Zipper all wore T-shirts and shorts with hiking boots. Charles and Max's Ts both were black with a Baltimore O's bird logo on them.

Zipper's T had a drawing of border collies herding sheep and on the front the words *The Blue Hill Fair 1984*. The boys had pale blue *Go Navy* hoodie sweatshirts tied around their waists. Zipper had tied the same woolen, long brown sweater she'd worn earlier that morning. *I guess she packs light,* Max thought.

Fred sat in the passenger seat. Around his neck was the strap to a brand-new case cradled like a baby in his hands, ready for photo ops with his new camera.

"Whatcha' got, Fred?" Pat asked.

"Birthday present from my loving bride: A Nikon N2000," said Fred.

"Whoa! Tops the camera lists for Best in '85!"

"I know. She told me to pick out what I wanted. I talked to a few newspaper photographers I know. This camera was their number one favorite, hands down."

"Picture this in *Time Magazine* or *Vacationer*—Fred's shots of 'Summer in Maine, 1985.' And to think I knew you before," Pat said to Fred. To those on the back seat of the truck he said, "Keep an extra eye out for Fred. We're in the land of eagles, osprey, loon, seals, harbor porpoise, porcupines . . . lots of other critters. When we get to the park and begin the hike, Fred and I'll do the head start . . . just to rest easy your minds, take guilt weight off your shoulders, leave behind all the 'Yes, teacher' stress far, far away. No worries you might scare away the 'Best in Show, Blue Ribbon Nature' shots," Pat said.

"Got it," Max said.

"For sure," said Charles.

"Loon and seals are a real possibility swimming in the bay or near tiny, offshore islands. You have an excellent chance to see wildlife when we take the shore trail," Zipper added.

"I'm psyched," said Fred.

"We're headed on Route 15 South to the Village of Deer Isle. It was incorporated in 1789," Pat told them. "From there I'll make a left on the Sunshine Road and into . . . no, I won't tell. I'll have you experience the 'wait for it' surprise."

Route 15 South is an uphill, down, round corner "Wow!" trip. They passed island salt water farms with two-hundred-year-old stone fences, lop-eared goats, giant work horses, long-necked white geese, and free-range wandering Rhode Island Red hens, who were often pecking seeds along the roadside. A *Slow Turkey Crossing* sign proved to be properly placed, for around a wild wooded bend in the road, there was a flock of wild turkeys.

Pat stopped the truck. Fred aimed his camera.

"Mama turkey and what hatched from this summer's clutch. Quiz time: anybody know what a group of wild turkeys is called? Hint: different from the name given to domesticated ones," Pat said.

"Ah, flock," said Charles.

"Group," said Zipper.

Max thought, then said, "Domesticated turkeys are called a gang or rafter, so I go with group or flock for the wild ones."

"You all get A+s," Pat said. "Now, let me up the bar, try out some turkey talk, while Fred gets his last photos. Here we go, Turkey Vocalizations, Animal Quiz level, hmm, 301."

"Gobble, gobble, cackle, cackle," Charles said, in a bored voice.

"Gobble, gobble, cluck, cluck, putt, putt, yelp." Max loved making animal sound words.

"Gobble, gobble, clack-clack-clack, cluck, putt-putt, yelp-yelps, cackles, kee-kees, kee-kees. Oh, and some whines," Zipper said.

"Excellent to all! But A ++ goes to Zipper. I'm guessing you've been listening to turkeys for some time," said Pat.

"Well, over the years we raised some . . . for Thanksgiving. One of the hardest learning experiences of my life. Fortunately, I'd gone off . . . wandering . . . when people came to pick their fresh-killed. Dad did the hard stuff," Zipper said.

"Oh no," Charles said, covering his ears a second too late.

"Sorry," said Max.

"It's what you do when you raise animals for table along with vegetable gardens," said Pat. "Okay, this will lighten things up. What do we call a group of seagulls?"

"Flock?" asked the boys.

"A colony," said Zipper.

"Another A+. Zip, good for you," said Pat. He looked out the windows. "Looks like these turkeys have it almost figured out. Oh, no, I'm wrong. Two decided to stand in the middle of the road. I guess they're expecting mama to tell them which way to go. Leaves us time for another question. What do we call a flock of crows, Zipper?"

"Ah, hmm, flock? I'm not sure."

"A murder!" answered the boys.

"Something Grandpa taught us," Max added.

"A murder? Oh no, gives me chills," said Zipper.

"But they're right. Remember, Zip, which state we're coming from and which city Edgar Allen Poe once lived in."

"Quoth the Raven, nevermore,'" recited Max. "Good ole Baltimore, Maryland."

All laughed.

"Okay, looks like the turkey trot has ended. All the Jennies and Jakes have found their mamas and decided to be a good little flock following her," said Pat. He turned the key and the engine roared, then he slipped the clutch into first gear and off they went again.

More woods, fields, then: "Telescope house, look left," Pat said. "See it? People added on as their families grew. Wonder why houses are attached to the barn? Upstate New York, Western Massachusetts, Connecticut, New Hampshire, Vermont, and Maine winters are harsh. During blizzards it's easier to feed animals when you can stay inside going from house through what is called an ell to the barn. Somewhere between house and barn used to be an outhouse. Now, of course, almost everyone has the luxury of a bathroom, but back less than seventy-five years ago, outhouses were still the usual place. Look! Over there, see that little white house. It's very old and see where the chimney is?"

"In the center of the house," Fred said.

"Yes. They're called center chimney Cape Cods. People started building them here in the early 1800s. Before that I guess people lived in little cabins as Deer Isle settlers arrived here as far back as 1762. Peter Powers, a Congregational minister, began visits in 1785, but Deer Isle town wasn't incorporated until 1789. Cape Cod homes with center chimneys became popular because a center chimney warmed the whole house; it was like one chimney was 'zoned heating' for many rooms. Very smart."

"Grandpa had our home in Maryland built that way," Max told Zipper.

They drove by newer homes, which stood out as not belonging. "Summer cottages," Zipper told Max and Charles.

Pat slowed the truck, made a left into a driveway, passing close to a sign that read: *Island Nursing Home / Rehabilitation and Pre-School Center.* He pulled into the parking lot.

"Why are we stopping here?" Charles asked.

"Well, I thought perhaps Zipper could give you two guys a quick tour of one of the most unique places on Deer Isle, or many other places I know of. It's a combination nursing, rehab and retirement home and children's center, where preschool children come for day care, beginner ABCs, numbers, and/or time away from home; a place to learn to socialize with children their own age and with all ages of adults. Very smart."

"Really?" Charles and Max asked in unison. They looked at each other and laughed.

"It happened again. You two really do respond like a guy duet," Pat said. "In this facility, elderly live and enjoy events with little children: puppet shows, sing-a-longs, story tellers, magic shows . . . imagine audiences, ages 2 to over 100 years. It has a family feeling, generations together, so to speak. Go check it out, guys. Zipper will be your tour guide."

Doors opened. All scrambled out of the truck. Pat and Fred stayed beside it. They were teachers who liked their students to learn from each other and make their own discoveries. Also, they needed time alone to carefully plan the day without Charles, Max, and Zipper near to overhear.

Zipper led the boys across the parking lot onto a zig-zagging path through flower beds to the front door. The air was filled the fragrance of peonies, roses, lilies . . . in all stages, and they were surrounded by buds opening and full feathery blooms in a dazzle of all colors against the blue-blue sky. Though neither boy would own up verbally to this shockingly beautiful garden, they were impressed.

Zipper pushed a blue square and a wide door slowly opened. "Watch out for the cats. They roam halls visiting anyone who might need a pet pal," Zipper said.

"Just cats?" Charles looked around the big brightly lit lobby. Cats were okay but he considered himself a dog person.

"Well, no dogs, except on special visiting days. Dogs trained to be quiet. We call them our Angel Dogs because they'll stretch out and listen as preschool children read to them, and almost all of them do not nod off and sleep, a big ego boost to a young child's self-esteem. One popular dog is a Golden Retriever named Love," Zipper told them.

"How do you know so much?" Max asked.

"Um, well, my mom volunteers here a few days a week. My dog is Love and she really does love to be read to."

"Whoa, how cool is that?" Charles exclaimed.

Zipper impressed Charles. Score, Max thought. As for Max, he'd been impressed with her ever since the beach. *I've never met a girl who acts . . . real and not fake. A girl I'm comfortable with. When I'm with most girls, I feel like I have to be some character in a play, or be a certain person . . . who's not me.*

"Okay, cats roam. Dogs visit and . . . ." He stopped and looked. "What are those tall, rounded top cages? See? Over there at the other end of the lobby?" Charles asked.

"Bird cages."

"What?"

"Well, several bird cages. Think of a village made of high-rise cages with talking birds in them."

Charles whistled a low, long, impressed whistle.

"Yep, they whistle, too," laughed Zipper.

"Do any talk?" asked Max.

"Actually, they do.

"Where'd they come from?" Charles asked.

"A few years ago a lady moved into the nursing home. She asked if she could bring her African Grey. Well, actually, she's always been generous to the Island, most especially to this home. The board of trustees discussed it and voted unanimously Yes! but with rules: the bird (later birds) must stay in the lobby and someone must be hired to feed, change water, and clean cages daily. Residents, owners of birds coming to live here, all must sign a contract: they are responsible for the cost of bird care and cage upkeep. A group of residents and homecare board members all sign the agreement."

"Interesting," Charles said. Max agreed.

"Okay. So let's greet the African Gray: Sgt. Pepper and his Lonely Hearts Club Band of pals in cages: Sam, a big white cockatoo and several parakeets. I forget their names. They just arrived."

To see "bird land," they had to go by a woman at the registration desk. As they walked near to her, she looked up and when she saw it was Zipper she waved.

"I brought two friends visiting from Maryland. I told them about the birds. We'll only be a minute. Mom's brother, Uncle Pat, is waiting for us in the parking lot," Zipper told her.

"Enjoy!" The woman smiled. "Just stop by or wave to me as you leave. Rules. You know how it is?"

"Yes, thanks," Max said.

"I've read where Great Grays have totally awesome vocabularies. They imitate animals and imitate exactly machine noises," Charles said.

"All true. Sgt. Pepper *is* amazing. He talks in sentences. Tells people how he's feeling; voices his opinion. He can make machine and animal sounds: phones ring, Westminster clock chimes, dogs barking. He also likes to give orders. His favorite is: 'Schools out, kids. Time to go home!'"

"Funny," the boys said.

Sgt. Pepper looked like a gray feather duster with bright eyes, beak, and skinny white legs, long toes, and nails. He greeted them by sounding a long-held note like a train whistle, then said, "And who do we have here now with my pal Zip?"

A real wow, but the wow turned into disbelief when Sgt. Pepper quizzed them: "Where are you from, young man? And you, older young man, where are you from? What's your age?" Then turning to the parakeets, he relayed to them perfectly all Max and Charles told him.

The parakeets conversed among themselves and then Sgt. Pepper asked them, "Where are you going today?"

"After we leave here, on a hike," Zipper told the bird.

"Pretty day. Elegant day! Get out of here! Get out, get out, get out, Zipper, Charles, and Max, as soon as you can. Scoot!"

Wide-eyed and with mouths open, too amazed to speak, Charles and Max turned heel and left, leaving Zipper to thank Sgt. Pepper for his time.

"Anytime, Doll Baby, you know how much I love you! Now go and join those two cuties. Woot-a-toot-toot!"

"Bye!" They said to the woman at the desk.

"Bye! Have a great day. Come back soon."

"Really cool!" Charles told Fred and Pat.

"So, Sgt. Pepper was in a welcoming mood? Glad to hear it." Pat said. "Okay, back in the truck. We have miles to go and things to see before we begin our hike."

Pat and Fred continued to talk camera talk. Topic: best places for nature shots. "Hope you're loaded up with film; there are many beautiful places on the hiking trail."

Meanwhile, on the back seat, Zipper and the boys talked animal tales.

"Sorry we didn't have time to look and see if Love was working today," Zipper said.

"Oh, that's okay. Seeing the birds was something else," Max said. "Another time we'll see Love."

"We have two dogs," began Charles.

"Well, actually, they belong to our grandparents. One is a beagle named Yappy, who spends his time napping on the roof of his doghouse or howling at the moon. He loves chasing rabbits when Grandpa lets him. But Grandpa never lets him off a lead or leash when the weather is warm in spring, summer, late September. Sometimes even into warm October because no one wants him to disturb nesting rabbits or to hurt their babies," Max said.

"The other dog, well, her whole name is F. Scott Fitzgerald, but we call her Fitz or Fitzgerald. She's an English Setter. I bet she'd make a great 'Read to Me' dog," Charles said.

"F. Scott Fitzgerald? Like the author of *The Great Gatsby,* right? But you said she? How did that happen? Or don't I want to know?" Zipper asked, looking not at Charles, but at Max.

Max smiled. "Let's just say it was a case of mistaken identity by the person whose turn it was to name the next puppy." Max raised his left palm and then, so Zipper could see but not Charles, put his right pointer finger into his palm and pointed to Charles. "But we all liked the name. It just sort of fits Fitz," Max said.

Zipper and Charles groaned at the pun.

"Have you read *The Great Gatsby* or watched the movie?" Max asked.

"Actually, yes. Both. I read it . . . I'm sort of an advanced reader, but math puzzles me. I used to attend the one-room Isle au Haut School. It's for grades K-8. Then our kid population dropped lower until it was down to six of us. One was Perri and one was me. The others were four- and five-year-olds. But on the island awesome college professors, writers, scientists, and artists live, many are semi or fully retired. My mom, who was teaching at the school back then, talked to the year-round professionals. A retired English professor-turned-writer tested my reading level. Now I go to her for literature, grammar, spelling, and creative writing. A physics professor is my math and physics teacher. My biology, chemistry, and marine science teacher is, well, it's my dad. Another woman,who's retired, is my history/ sociology/ psychology teacher. During summers, I learn about archaeology and Egyptology from a university professor who summers on the island. For religion I have Pastor Ed, who is a minister with Maine Seacoast Mission. Every weekend, he and the crew of a large ship visit all the island churches, even the ones 25 miles or more offshore. Tiny churches on tiny islands are filled with mostly seacoast fishing people. Because of weather and other reasons, Pastor Ed contacts them when he's near shore; someone rings the church bell. When the bell rings, people gather in the church; in winter, someone is picked to start the wood stove. There's no real set time for church to begin due to wind, whitecaps, and the tides. Sorry, that was long-winded, but Pastor Ed is amazing.

"Anyway, as for gym and sports, I'm a rock-hopper mostly, but I do play a mean game of tennis. Two pros who summer on the island work with me. We have an intergenerational lacrosse, basketball, and volleyball team . . . we challenge church and school groups when they arrive every fall, spring, and summer for overnight tours. As for music, I've played piano ever since I could reach the keys. I love it. I play classical, swing, show tunes, Beatles, folk. A few years ago I started studying violin. I play with a Celtic quartet. I draw, paint, keep a journal. . . .

"But, your question. Yes, I read *The Great Gatsby,* then saw the movie. I rather read than watch. When I read a story, the pictures appear and the voices of characters are loud in my head. The way I see and hear them doesn't always match a movie script or what is projected on the large screen. Do you understand? Talk, talk, talk . . . I must sound like some word geek."

All the stuff Zipper tells us teaches us what life is really like when you're twelve and live on an island in Maine. Out loud Max said, "You're no geek. It sounds like you get all kinds of stuff we get at home but without waiting until you test into a certain grade. And you don't have to breathe gasoline fumes as you wait in car pool lines. And that's a good thing."

"Awesome life. . . . I have questions," Charles said.

"Ask away." She leaned back against the truck's cushioned seat, combing her long hair with her fingers.

She's the Cheshire Cat from Alice in Wonderland . . . . Look at that smile, Max thought.

"Okay, wait, wait, don't tell me . . . just kidding," said Charles.

Max smirked.

While the back seat youth chatted about animals and the nursing home, Pat turned onto the Sunshine Road. They passed homes with boats, signs such as *Henry's Lobsters for Sale*, a veterinary hospital, the Deer Isle ambulance and fire company.

"Hey! Guys and Zip! You on the back seat. Open your windows and enjoy this view," Pat said.

They rolled down windows. Seconds later, Pat slowed, pulling into a scenic overlook. He stopped the truck and shut the engine off.

"Chill time. The park is a few miles away, but Fred needs to take pictures of this spot. A friend of mine calls it Paradise Cove. I think he's right. At high tide and midtide, like right now, I think it could be Paradise, minus a journey across Dante's River Styx or an interview with Saint Pete."

All exited the stuffy, cramped truck space, glad to stretch. Pale green grassy fields and hay swayed behind them; in front towering evergreens with shaggy boughs, were giants touching the sky. Beyond, shaped like a huge letter *S,* blue salt tides were lazily filling over sun-warmed mud, and waves were coming closer to edges where shore grasses began. The only sounds around them were the breezes through tree boughs, a lone seagull cry, and their interior rhythms: heartbeat "lub-dub" and in-out breathing.

Fred moved from one photo spot to the next.

Charles flopped in the long grass. Zipper and Max walked further down the Sunshine Road toward the next curve in Paradise Cove.

After Paradise Cove, what more? Max wondered. *This is really pretty.*

Max soon discovered Paradise Cove was an entrance to many experiences yet to be.

After a rest in Paradise, Pat drove on a single lane into the woods on dirt, grass, and brown pine needles, with pull-outs, should other vehicles exit, as they entered. A mile, two miles into the dense woods with all windows down, sea salt, and balsam-scented air surrounded them. At a cut in the woods, they saw a wooden shingle; in the middle of it was painted a black *P.* Here Pat maneuvered the truck over roots, pine needles, moss, around rocks, between stumps, and into the parking space, which was wide enough to hold two medium-size cars or one truck.

"We're here. Once we're inside the Preserve, there's an information stand. I can tell you from years of being here, follow the single slash marks on trees, rocks, even on fallen logs. They're called blazes, and they're made to guide hikers and keep them on trails. When you see a *Shore Path* sign, take it. Fred and I will meet you at a pink granite beach. Zip, you know where I mean?" Pat asked.

"Indeed," she said.

Charles was about to bolt.

Pat said, "But, before we split, wait a moment." He went to the truck's hatch and pulled out his pack. He undid a strap and from inside one pouch pulled out a brown paper bag. He relocked the strap and shouldered his pack. He closed and locked the truck, then returned to them.

"Give us a 10- minute start. Have a snack. If you need to bathroom . . . well, this is the wilderness," Pat said. He reached into his brown sack, and dramatically took . . . .

"Here's one for each of you: little trowels, brand new, never used. Consider it a birthday present for my August birthday friends and family," he smiled. "In case you, ah, need to dig a hole. I trust you three to obey environment-friendly rules. Oh, yes, and good friends keep watch when a pal needs privacy, warns them when danger or other hikers might appear. Have fun," said Pat.

"I mean, really. . . ?" Charles asked, looking down at a new little red-handled trowel.

"Mine has a blue handle and Zipper's . . . ."

"Purple—my favorite color. Good news, guys! The price tags on all three are clean and white. Meaning these trowels *are* brand-new. Never used. Uncle Pat is a very practical guy. He thinks of everything." Zipper opened her pack and shoved her trowel in.

"We can use it for other things, Charles. Don't be so single-focused," Max said as he stored his trowel in his pack.

"I guessssss. Oh, yeah. I've got an idea. Back home in Maryland it'll be good for scraping in search of arrowheads,

66

should we have an archaeological dig. I need to nudge Grandpa about that."

Things would be okay for Charles; now he had a plan to think about. He stored his trowel in his pack.

"There are arrowheads where your Grandpa lives?" Zipper asked.

"Oh, yeah, on The Property—what we call the farm we live on. It's a farm with lots of woods. It is where our Grandpa grew up. It was where an ancient tribe of Native American Indians lived: the Woodlands. Grandpa has the 'eye' and finds stone artifacts all the time," Charles said.

"Really?"

"Yep. When he works the soil tilling his big vegetable garden . . . . Your Uncle Pat uses some of our garden space to raise vegetables in," Max said.

"Really?"

"Yep. Anyway, often Grandpa walks down the rows in the garden, looking at the fresh-tilled earth, especially after it rains. Then, he sees them: bird points, arrowheads, spears, and scrapers. Most are in the garden. Some are in the streams."

"Wow."

"Pottery, too. Little squares, all the size of . . . . Actually, they look like . . . if you made your own tile for a Scrabble game . . . made it out of dough, adding little bits of a soft stone called soapstone. If you baked it and if it puffed up about a quarter inch then, bingo. Grandpa says soapstone pottery was a primitive type," Max said. *I think I impressed her,* he thought and felt warm inside.

"Maybe someday I'll visit Uncle Pat and Aunt Popee in Maryland. In Maine, we have lots of Native American History and historical sites where people find arrowheads, spears . . .

many other things. We have four tribes: the Micmacs, way up in Aroostook County, Maliseet near Houlton; the Passamaquoddy and Penobscot are more spread out."

"We have no living tribes left in Maryland, even though many people do have Native American ancestors." Charles was impressed. "Later you'll have to tell me the names you just said again, and I'll write them down. Can people go places to see and hear others telling about their heritage stuff? Like reenactments? Story tellers? People living their story?"

"Sure. You can't? How sad." Zipper reached into her backpack. She took out her water jar, bread, fruit, and nuts. "We'll give Fred and Uncle Pat a few more minutes while we're talking. Snack time."

Max began opening his pack.

"Good idea." Charles opened his. "Oh, and here's my pad and pencil. Zipper, if you could repeat those tribe names, I'll copy them down."

She did.

He did.

"You can find arrowheads here, too. Right here where we are now. There're many other spots not far away. Maybe your folks or Uncle Pat and Popee can take you. The ancient Indian tribe known as the Red Paint People lived in various parts of Maine. Some lived on the shores of Blue Hill Bay, only 30 minutes from here. People find all kinds of arrowheads, scrapers, and what they call 'lucky stones.' Like your Woodland tribes, they left much behind and have been gone a long time."

Being with Zipper is like being in a library, only she's not as stuffy, Max thought.

68

Ten minutes later, Max, Charles and Zipper had finished their snacks and started the hike. They believed they'd given Fred and Pat enough of a head start.

They walked a few hundred feet across a grassy lawn, then Zipper directed them to a large wooden sign. On it, each trail was described and identified with colored blazes. There was an arrow where to start each trail. The blazes were blue or double blue (one slash mark topping the other). They had a choice, but Zipper knew which choice to make: "We'll take the shore trail first, then the path into the woods. Follow the single blue blazes."

They walked through the field on the mown path, now worn to dusty earth by the footsteps of other hikers. It was, after all, nearly mid-August.

As they walked, Zipper pointed out different wildflowers. Many were the same as those filling fields in Maryland: Black-eyed Susan, Queen Anne's lace, wild daisies, and (just beginning) purple asters. Seeing these flowers made both boys feel "at home."

The path angled left away from the field and into the woods; it dropped down into a low, wet marsh where, in some places, boards had been placed to walk on. These boards were flat and fat like balance beams in gym class but resting on mud. Sometimes there were two boards, other times only one that was less than eight inches wide.

On their right side, hardwoods became fewer and fewer as pines and firs took over. Ground pine and tiny saplings mixed with many kinds of moss: bright green, blue gray, white gray.

"See there?" Zipper asked. "See the light gray moss? It's called reindeer moss. Can you see antlers?"

Both boys looked.

I see ghost reindeer, Max thought, *but I'll never say* that *out loud.*

On their left, trees thinned until soon they were out of the woods and standing on pink granite ledge several yards from bay waters. Across the bay were small islands: some looked like piles of rock with no more than two or three evergreens growing on them. In the bay waters were lobster markers and moorings, which looked like big black or white balls. Here large lobster boats, sailboats, or cabin cruisers tied up as summer sailors and lobster folk took little dinghies to shore. It was very quiet, postcard pretty, and the fragrance of sea salt and balsam almost overwhelming.

They sat down on the sun-warmed, huge, flat pink granite ledges, which sloped down to the sandy bay beach.

"I bet Fred's snapping one picture after another," Charles said.

"Good. Then when we're home, we can look at his pictures and live today all over again."

"Ugh, too sweet, Max. A Valley Girl would say, 'Gag me with a spoon,'" Charles moaned.

"What's a Valley Girl?" Zipper asked.

"You've really never heard that expression?" Charles asked.

"Well, we live sort of away from . . . ah, what would you call it. . . ." Zipper was not sure what a proper 1980s pop label for her home and lifestyle was.

"Um, maybe we could say you live about thirty years in the past and not in the hip 1980s pop culture," Max said. "Valley Girl is a label. It means . . . . Well, okay, you know how Toni was dressed this morning and how she acts?"

"Like a magazine model. This morning she acted like she was at least 180 degrees different from me."

70

"Right. Perfect. Well, Toni *is* a Valley Girl. They have their own clothes style and their own slang. They say things like, ah," his mind went blank . . . . "Help me, Charles."

"Ooh, let's do lunch!" Charles said in a high-pitched voice. "Like that would be so fresh, for sure. Lots of Valley Girls are mall chicks, who want to 'Like, shop till we drop' and think those of us who like nature, enjoy hiking, and outside stuff are lame, or worse, we are 'grody to the max'—but not our Max. We are totally uncool whereas hanging around dress shops is 'Ohmygod, so rad.' They're just a bunch of wannabes and have no idea how 'wicked good' this nature thing really is."

Max applauded his brother.

Zipper shook her head. "I don't think any of those expressions have made it to Isle au Haut," she said.

"Good!" Charles did a fist bump.

"Or, we could just do a . . . double thumbs into the air," Max said and did it.

"Well, time to get back to trail walking. Careful, sometimes this trail can trip you up," Zipper said.

It wasn't easy to look away from the bay, to stop staring at the water and rocky islands, to stop searching for sea life. And too, the manmade beauty of well-crafted wooden boats: rowboats, cruisers, fishing boats, and the new Hinckley three-masted sailboat rocking on its mooring.

Now, they followed Zipper's instructions, walking in almost silence. Each was thinking his/her thoughts as they soaked in the beauty of bay-beside-forest. Being quiet helped them to concentrate as each foot step counted; each had to be set in a firm place where it would not slip or slide on loose gravel or trip over one of the hundreds of snaking roots crossing the path in all kinds of shapes and angles. As they followed the path, woods side, they saw not only trees but many large patches of moss.

On this warm day, salty sea water mixing with balsam created a pungent, sweet fragrance, but as the path moved deeper into the woods, salty air mixed with the sharp smell of "nurse" trees.

Nurse trees were trees that had fallen and were slowly rotting into the ground. Some had fallen many years ago. They now looked like rounded earth masses covered in moss and lichen. Younger nurse trees, those that had fallen only a few years before, were fuzzy with moss, lichen, and ground pine. Growing from the heartwood of the nurse trees were big and small shoots, new saplings, many different kinds of hardwoods like oak, maple and birch, and all varieties of evergreens. The nurse trees' rotting richness nurtured all.

On the shore path hike, they stepped carefully, taking timeouts to look for sea creatures. They'd seen gulls, loons, geese, and cormorant, but no seals. Twenty minutes into the hike, they reached a 45-degree climb consisting of stone, tree roots, pine needles, fallen trees, and earth-covered banks. As they started this climb, they saw a very old, no longer smelly lobster claw rammed onto a broken pine branch and, like an arrow, it was pointing up.

"Look, a 'guiding light claw.' Maybe Pat or Fred left it," Max said. "See, it's pointing to a lookout spot, away from the double blue blazes to single blue ones."

All three climbed the steep incline. From its very top, they looked down onto a small cove and a beach filled with pink granite pebbles. Zipper pointed and there they saw Fred and Pat with shoes and socks off, resting on beach towels.

The kids looked for footholds, but at times it was an "on your bottom slide" down. In less than 5 minutes, they reached the beach where the men were sitting.

"No trouble finding us?" Pat asked.

"A certain lobster claw on a certain branch helped," Charles said.

Pat laughed.

"I took a picture of it. I mean, how could we ever explain a claw marker to the others?" Fred asked.

"Someone we know might say: 'Like, look, do some trees grow red claws up here? Grody to the max!' or something like that," Charles said in his best Valley Girl imitation.

"Bad, Charles, bad," Fred said. He laughed so hard he started to cough. He grabbed his water bottle and took a drink. "You all need to cool your feet. Wade in. Or swim if you dare. It's bay water and it's cold, but warmer now in August than any other time in the year."

Max, Charles, and Zipper shed hiking boots, socks, sweaty shirts, sweaters. They took off layers until they were wearing only their bathing suits.

"Ouch. Ouuuch! Ow!" Charles said, walking across the rough and wobbling stones to the lapping tide waters.

"Oh, yeah, forgot to warn you, beach stones are hard on your soles," Pat said.

"Hmm." Max looked at Pat. *He's testing us the way Grandpa sometimes does. I'll take the challenge; put my mind on something besides my feet.* He stood on the pink stones and yes, it was painful, but Max wasn't going to cave. "I'm going for brave new guy from Maryland." He walked to the water's edge. Yes, it was colder than pools at home but really not too bad. Where water lapped against the beach there was more sand than stone. It was easier to walk on gravelly sand than the inch-size, rough-edged granite pebbles.

"Hey, Max, good for you!" Fred said. He snapped a picture recording the moment for all time.

Zipper soon stood beside him.

Charles gingerly slow-stepped across the stones.

"If you can stand the cold water—and it's really not too bad today with the sun beaming down—there's a cave we can wade to, maybe swim into. It's to our left," Zipper said.

"Lead on," Max said.

Zipper waded in until the water was to her hips, then she made a shallow dive and swam three yards or more to her left. She began treading water and waved to Max. "It's really not cold or deep. I'm treading water because I'm afraid the bottom might be slimy with rockweed."

"Okay, here goes nothing," Max said. He also made a shallow dive into the cold. Yes! It was cold, but not bitterly so. Soon he was by Zipper's side. "It's a cave. Charles, it's a cave! Not deep and not scary but a cave. Are you going to come in and see it?"

"Think I'll pass," Charles said as began inching back. His mind was set on sunbathing on one of the beach towels Fred had spread for them. "Fred, did you bring the sun lotion?"

"Yep." Fred tossed the bottle to Charles.

"Pat, do you see something over on that island? The one directly across from us? Looks like a dramatic nature event has begun," Fred said. He reached for his camera and began attaching his zoom lens.

"Yes, I see it. Nobody make a noise. Zip and Max, soon as you finish inspecting that cave, swim to the right, climb to where ledge stones are wide and warm. Once out, look to the

74

treeless island directly across the bay and in front of this beach. We think something is happening there."

"Huh?" Charles asked. He stopped spreading True Hawaii Coconut Cream on his face, arms, legs, neck, and skinny body.

Zipper and Max were swimming the sidestroke. They looked like seals; within moments they had climbed the great flat pink granite ledges.

"Oh, sun-warmed stone feels amazing," Max sighed. He rested, placing as much of his chilled flesh as possible on the hot rock.

Zipper sat a few feet away. Her attention was on the rocky island in the distance. "Yes, Uncle Pat, I can see it clearly from here. If you climb the boulders on this side, be careful, it's a little steep. Not bad. You can do it. Over here I think you'll have a better view. Uncle Pat, you didn't bring your binoculars?"

"Of course I did," Pat said, pulling clothes and bags of food from his pack. Seconds later he triumphantly raised a black case. He opened it, pulled free his binoculars. "*Voila!*"

"Man oh, man. What a show! Not a happy one. Nature doesn't always give us happy endings," Pat said.

"Yes."

"Can you see where a large tree trunk washed up? On it there's a. . . ."

"Bald eagle!" Fred said.

"And he's, ah, doing what . . . ?" asked Charles.

"He's feasting on something," said Fred.

From far away, they began to hear faint screams that became louder and turned into piercing cries, angry calls. They could see an eagle being surrounded by a frenzy of white and gray bodies, which began diving closer and closer.

Seagulls going after an eagle? Max wondered. Then he heard Zipper whispering beside him.

"The eagle killed one of the gulls. Now it's eating it in front of them. The colony of seagulls is enraged. The dead gull may have been a friend . . . or family."

"I never knew seagulls would band against an eagle. I always thought they were silly birds until today. First, this morning with the crows, then on the beach where they were sneaky, and now this . . . this . . . war against an eagle," Max said. He was impressed.

"They are getting bolder and bolder," said Pat, watching through his binoculars. "The eagle is starting to lose his cool. This may have a pretty nasty ending, not that it's a pretty sight right now."

"But an important learning experience for Charles and Max," Fred said.

"Yeah," Pat said, "and a refresher course for all of us."

Once Max thought how he'd seen a "nature event" which upset him so much, he never told Charles about it. *But back then, Charles was only eight. Now he's nine. I trust Fred and Pat know how old a kid should be to witness tough nature things; things Grandpa calls Scary; how certain kinds of Scary are good lessons helping us to learn as we get older.*

Zipper turned to Max. "It might get gory. I know because I've seen things like this before. Can you handle it? Can Charles?"

"I think I can. In May, I saw what happened when a crayfish thought he could win against a giant bullfrog, but I never told Charles," Max said.

"At your home?"

"Grandpa's pond."

"You'll have to tell me about it later," Zipper said.

76

"I will. But this. . . ."

"Are we going to watch some seagulls and an eagle all day?" Charles asked.

"Are you watching, Charles?" Fred asked.

"Oh, now and then, I guess. But how long will we be hanging out here?"

"A few more minutes, maybe 10 or 15. We have lots of time," said Pat. "You can set the alarm on your watch if you wish."

"Okay," said Charles, turning back to face the beach and resting his head on the fuzzy soft beach towel. "You go ahead and do your spy-on-nature thing and I'll do what I want to."

"Okay," said Fred. "Sounds good." He adjusted the zoom on his Nikon.

"I think Charles is going to miss this nature moment, too," Zipper whispered to Max.

"Probably a good thing, but we aren't, are we?" He looked at the tall, slim girl beside him who sat watching the eagle and seagull colony. *She's so cool,* he thought.

"I've seen it before, many times. Each time I see something like this, I learn more from it. This time, I think, if you need to... ah . . . what's that term, oh, yeah, *debrief;* if you need to debrief, I'll be here for you."

"Thanks, sounds like a plan."

The eagle continued eating: reaching down, pulling, and dramatically flourishing pieces of flesh and bone, while sea breezes sent white and gray feathers into the air. *Is the eagle's shameless mockery causing the other gulls to be bolder?* Max wondered.

"Look at the gulls now!" Fred said.

Everyone looked but Charles who continued to ignore what was happening. He was reading his book.

Several seagulls pecked at the eagle's lowered head each time he grasped more of the kill in his beak.

"It looks like they're attacking him in rhythm. Imagine if this was a movie we were watching, I wonder what background music producers would pick?" Max said.

Zipper shrugged.

"Maybe something we can work on. My mind is totally swept up in . . . . Look! The eagle just took a swipe at one of the bolder ones. A miss. The gull is back and the eagle is ready for him."

Max couldn't believe what he was watching. A puff of white feathers burst from a diving seagull. Halo-like, they appeared to hang in the sky. The gull faltered, lost its rhythm, and the eagle struck again, this time a fatal blow. The gull fell crashing onto pink ledge not far from where the eagle perched. Other gulls continued to take turns battling. They never faltered. They swiped the bald eagle's head and pulled eagle feathers free.

"A triumph," Zipper said.

"Look!" said Max. More and more gulls, encouraged by the sight of shed eagle feathers, attacked the eagle's white head. As the eagle lifted its head away from its kill, stretched its neck, more and more gulls came at him, claws first, making inflight pauses, similar to how Max, Charles, and Zipper had watched them that morning when they dropped mussels.

"Phew!" Pat whistled.

"Wish I was videotaping this. Oh, well. I'll just keep snapping," Fred said.

"Believe me, even a simple series of stills will jolt this scene back should your memory fade. Look now."

Everyone saw the dramatic finish, with the exception of Charles, who was resting belly down on a beach towel, back turned, head bowed, eyes on his book.

The eagle, who had been bombarded by at least twenty-five angry seagulls, left its fresh kill and, with the body of the first gull held firmly in its talons, spread his wide wings, lifted up, and flew into the woods, low to the ground, headed to the trail Pat and the group had just hiked. Several gulls followed as if giving chase but only as far as the woods, then they circled back, returning to the pink ledge, scene of the "murder." Some landed. Others continued flying until they were out of sight. A few inspected the body of the gull killed while attacking the eagle.

"I guess the drama is over," Pat said. "Time to regroup and continue our hike. We have a cemetery to see." He climbed down from the high observation site.

"Sounds good to me," Fred said, returning his zoom lens to the black camera bag and placing it in his backpack. He crawled down to the pink stony beach.

Max and Zipper, who didn't have as far to go, were soon sitting on beach towels. They were silent. Both reflected on the drama they'd witnessed. They pulled shorts and T-shirts over swimsuits. Due to the saltiness of the bay waters, each took out bottled water and drank.

Charles continued to read. Was he ignoring them or intrigued by his book?

Max's patience was short. Finally, he asked as calmly as he could, "Charles, what are you reading that's so fascinating?"

Charles looked up at Max. He saw Zipper, Pat, and Fred looking at him.

"Information on the American bald eagle," he calmly said.

Max's mouth dropped open. He shook his head in disbelief. Took a deep breath and then asked, "So what have you learned?"

"Bald eagles are called the *apex predators*. They were picked to symbolize the United States in 1787 because they're birds with authority. The U.S. was not the first country to choose them as their symbol. Long ago, when the Romans were powerful, the eagle was the symbol of Rome." Charles looked over to Zipper. "And you should like this: the female is the bigger of the two."

"The female is the ruler of the nest?" Max said.

"And what is the nest called? I used to know?" Zipper asked. She flopped on a beach towel, stretched, bounced into a sitting position, and began pulling on her hiking boots.

"Weird word, so yeah, easy to forget. Nests are called *eyries*. They're built high in trees or on cliffs. This is something I'm really struggling with as it just doesn't seem like the best way for eagles to have good numbers when it comes to population. The female lays two eggs. Both male and female are good parents, taking turns keeping the eggs warm and hunting for food. But once the eggs are hatched, get this . . . the older, larger, dominant chick will kill its sibling. And that's the female! She kills her baby brother. And get this . . . the real clincher, the parents let it happen."

"Whoa. Heavy stuff, Charles," Pat said.

"Really," said Max.

"Does it say how long eagles live? Or how heavy a snack they can carry home," Fred asked.

"Yeah, it does. Average age of a bald eagle in the wild is 15-20 years. Those in captivity will live much longer. In fact, one eagle lived into its mid- 40s. As far as strong, their killer claws can carry something weighing up to about 4 pounds."

"Great facts to know, Charles," Zipper said.

They all agreed.

"Where did you get this book? Was it back at the house?" Fred asked.

"No, actually, it was offered for free. . . ."

"Don't tell," Max said, "not. . . ."

"Yep, it was something I picked up where I got all those other cool brochures back at the Maine Visitors' Center." Charles closed the little book. He looked at the others. "Pretty cool, huh?"

"Yea, pretty cool, Charles," Fred said.

"Did you guys see anything interesting happen with an eagle offshore on those rocks?" Charles asked, looking from face to face.

"Ah, we'll tell you later," Pat said.

"Yep, for now better repack and dress. We have a cemetery to check next," said Fred.

Chapter 5
Hiking in Paradise

Part 2:
Stories from Stones

C harles, Max, Zipper, Fred, and Pat arrived at an intersection in the trail where the single blue blazes they were following joined with double blue. Here they also saw two red arrows pointing in opposite directions. Single blue would lead them to The Cemetery, their destination. To get there would require turning away from the glittering blue bay and entering a thick growth of pine and cedars, where moss thickly covered the ground and nurse trees. Several hundred feet later a narrow earthen trail became a wider, sandy path: an old road bed.

Fred, Pat, and their youthful companions saw the blue slash marks and followed them.

"See the stones . . . an old stone fence?"

Nods.

"Yep."

"Yes, sir."

"Hmm?"

"Well, once upon a time this land was a farm," Pat said.

Fred took some photographs, then put his camera away. He began examining the stones.

Pat was interested in stone fences and workmanship done over two hundred years ago. Both men began to study how the builders of this wall fit stones together without use of cement or modern adhesives.

"Why are we stopping here?" Charles asked. "This isn't The Cemetery."

82

"Good fences make good neighbors," said Pat. "Anyone, age nine or twelve years, recognize that phrase from a famous poem? Couple of hints: the poet lived in many places, but mostly New Hampshire. Second hint: the poet won the Pulitzer Prize for poetry . . . . more than once. Yet at the start of this poet's career, American publishers sent poems back with rejection slips again and again. The poet traveled to England and was published there. In England, two books of poetry were published and the author became popular almost immediately. On his return to America after a few years in England, everyone wanted to publish this poet's poems. One publisher reprinted the two books that had been published in England and continued to publish everything this poet wrote. Third hint: the name of this poem has the word *walls* in it. Do I hear any guesses?" Pat asked.

I know, thought Max, *but I'll wait for Zipper and Charles.*

"In third grade, we had to memorize her poem. It began something like, 'I'm a Nobody and are you a Nobody, too', I think," Charles said perkily.

Max hid his face in his hands and groaned.

"No, Charles, that's a poem by Emily Dickinson," Zipper said. "This poem was written by a man. The name of the poem is 'Mending Wall' and Max," she turned to Max who was standing a few feet behind her watching Pat and Fred examine the round granite stones, "Max, who wrote it? I bet you know?"

"Robert Frost," Max said. "'Mending Wall' appeared in his second book of poetry: *North of Boston.* No sweat. We studied Frost for about a month last year."

"Bravo!" said Pat. "Okay, any idea why Frost and his family went to England? What year they went? What year he returned? The American publisher who became his publisher for the rest of his career?"

"Like, geez, Pat, now I feel like I'm in summer school," Charles moaned.

"A bit of history; a bit of literature," Max said. "I love it. Let's see. I think Frost was a farmer, but not a good one. I think he farmed in New Hampshire in . . . . not sure what the name of the town was. He and his family left for England when they failed at farming. I guess maybe they thought the English might enjoy poems by someone who was a descendant of the first colonists."

"Good job. Zipper, any additions before I fill in with biography fun facts?" Pat asked. As he asked this question and listened for an answer, he discovered a place where several stones had rolled free into thick weeds and were partially embedded in the ground. He began working one stone free. Fred saw him and the two worked together to loosen one stone and then another. They stopped each time one of the kids spoke. They were "multitask" teachers who respected what young people had to say.

"The family went to England after failing farming on land bought for them by his grandfather, who lived in Lawrence, Massachusetts," Zipper said. "Frost was actually born in San Francisco, but his father died of tuberculosis when Frost was eleven and his mom took him and his sister, Jeanie, back to live in Lawrence. Later he married Elinor White, his high school sweetheart, after she earned her college degree. By the way, Frost attended Dartmouth and Harvard, but dropped out of both schools."

Applause.

"Dates? Do we have dates?" Pat asked as he and Fred silently tried to figure out how and where the stones they'd found were to be replaced in the rock wall.

"Okay, okay. Dates, I do dates," said Charles. "Judging by who we're talking about, the name of the poem, and trip to England, I'm guessing: Frost and family went to England before WWI. That was the place and the time to make connections. When the war started, I'm betting, as a father of several children, Frost and family came back to America quick as they could. Dates: let's say they sold the farm about 1912, went to England shortly afterwards. Frost met people who saw what a gifted poet he was. They gave him a head start. Then the war broke out. Unlike some American college men and women, who believed joining up might be a thrill and who left school to enlist in the Great War, Frost didn't enlist nor did he stay in Europe. I'm going to guess, Frost and family were back in America by 1915?"

"The Numbers Star has hit the mark!" Pat said. "Bingo! By 1915, Frost *was* back in America with two books of poetry published in England. Almost immediately, those two books were republished by Henry Holt. The Frost family was now set. They bought a home in the small New Hampshire town of Franconia near the White Mountains. Frost enjoyed his writing life. Now a published poet, he began his poetry reading circuit at Dartmouth where, as a student, he'd only lasted one month. He gave poetry readings and guest lectures at the University of Michigan and Harvard, but Amherst College became one of his favorite colleges. He taught there for forty-five years. During his summers he went to Middlebury, Vermont, where he taught English. He won his first Pulitzer Prize for poetry in 1924."

"He was a slow bloomer, but when it all happened, it happened quickly. When we study poetry in schools, we always learn a poem by Frost," said Max.

"I doubt you are asked to memorize 'Mending Walls,' but teachers often have students read it and spend some time studying it," said Fred.

He tried placing his stone into a gaping hole. Pat added his but the fit wasn't quite right. Not yet.

"True, Fred. I think the Frost poem most students must memorize is 'The Road Not Taken.' We had to study it last year. We had to write about it as it appears and as it's understood metaphorically . . . . ah, Charles that translates as *symbolically*. For instance: choosing one career over another; the one career being the road not taken," Max explained.

"Max, you're sounding more and more like a writer," Charles said. "And that's a good thing."

"Thanks, Charles, from you that's a great compliment! So, back to the poem. By taking the road less taken, we'll end up . . . . at a cemetery! Eventually," said Max. He laughed and so did Charles and Zipper.

All three turned to watch the men trying to mend the wall.

Fred and Pat exchanged stones. Each tried fitting his stone in the open space, shifting stones back and forth.

"May I try?" Charles asked.

"Sure," said Fred and Pat.

Charles stepped close to the wall. He looked at it from both sides. Then he took one stone, gave it back. Took the other stone, examined it, and gave it back. Finally, he guided first Pat's stone to a certain area of the wall but did not allow Pat to let go or fit it in. Next, he did the same with Fred. When both stones were inches from the gaping hole, Charles

86

said, "Try moving toward the hole both at the same time; don't change the stone's position yet; lead with the stone, not your hands."

They did as Charles instructed. Stopped when he asked them to; readjusted and then:

"*Voila!*" Pat said. The two stones fit in like a glove.

"Guess I'll have to read 'Mending Wall,'" Charles said.

All applauded Charles, who looked humble and simply said. "It was like a puzzle."

Pat quoted from the poem "Mending Wall":

"We have to use a spell to make them balance:

'Stay where you are until our backs are turned!'

We wear our fingers rough with handling them."

The five began walking again, following the old stone wall. Three or four minutes went by, then Fred said, "Look, see? Here we are." He pointed to a fenced-in area almost hidden by green wild bush growth and an orchard of old apple trees.

By an unspoken agreement, silence seemed best.

They separated to look at each stone in The Cemetery. There were few and all were worn. Only the deepest letter/number cuts and shapes were easily discernible. Max and Charles traced inscriptions with their fingertips; they could feel the words and numbers, but by making a rubbing, they would be able to read what was written on the stones.

Fred and Pat handed out paper and distributed crayons. Zipper, Charles, and Max began their stone rubbings. Often they needed help from each other: one or two people firmly holding the paper flat and taut against the stone while the other rubbed a crayon back and forth. The places where letters were almost lost were still hollows and not colored by the crayons. Those hollows became words not seen when looking at the stone. Each rubbing was labeled and signed at the bottom by the person who had selected and rubbed that stone.

The Cemetery was one of the quietest places the boys had ever been. It was not scary. Or if it was, it was "Scary" by Grandpa's definition: it was truly a "teaching Scary," a good "Scary."

While the young people worked rubbing stones, Pat moved around the little cemetery plot sketching and scribbling names and dates of people buried there. Meanwhile, Fred took pictures of each stone. The rubbings and the written particulars would be shared with the family later, along with the significance of gravestone symbols and why they were carved on gravestones during the 1800s when many of these stones had been placed here.

When everyone was ready, one by one, they left The Cemetery. Zipper was the last to go. Her back was turned to the others as she placed wildflowers on all the graves and spent silent time at each one. She stayed the longest and placed the most flowers on one particular grave.

They regrouped around Pat beside the trail marker.

"When will we share our rubbings with each other?" Charles asked.

"It will happen sometime later today while still light or when . . . truly night."

"Now, let me go over some instructions for the rest of this hike: it is to be done alone, one by one, in silence," Pat said. "Follow the single blue blazes to the field. You'll recognize it when you get there. It's where we began the hike, except instead of going into the woods, we went left down the shore path. The field will not appear immediately. First go through an old growth of trees, lots of thick mossy spots, wet places with boards to walk on. We'll meet you back at the truck. Since Fred is taking 'memory' photographs, he'll go first. I'll be last. The rest of you are sandwiched in the middle. Space yourselves out and remember: Not a peep."

Fred added, "To be specific, each person begins walking the trail after giving the person ahead of him/her a 10-minute start. This, hopefully, will give each of you time to explore places that interest you most. I believe each of us will find something, some place we wish to spend time looking at, thinking about, wondering why, how, what, when, or maybe even who."

"Depending on how quickly we take this last part of the trail, we should arrive back to the truck in 30 to 45 minutes. The truck is our meeting place. From there we load in and go join the rest of the family, keeping closely to our schedule," Fred said.

Each found a place to sit. Water bottles came out. It was now late morning. They had done so much already and it wasn't even noon.

Walking this section of the hike alone might seem easy to some, silly to others or "Scary." Knowing someone was ahead and someone behind you, helped ease the "Scary."

One by one, each entered the dark, shadowy forest of old-growth trees. This particular forest had never been harvested for wood. Some trees, hundreds of years old, towered over their heads. They passed the greenest moss they'd ever seen. Bending down, touching it, they discovered how very soft it was, soft enough to sleep on. *To sleep on a moss bed would be like sleeping on the softest of soft mattresses. Had anyone ever done that? And if so, what had they dreamed?* Max thought.

His imagination was a jumble of images. He knew, once he opened his journal, his hand would ache by the time he finished trying to describe all of what he had experienced already this day. He would write about this last hike alone through these woods. And he would write in great detail. *I think Pat and Fred were wise to make us take this part of the hike, alone and in silence. Would we have seen as much, felt things as deeply, if we were talking with each other or near each other or even close enough to hear someone else's footsteps, breath, sighs, yawns? I doubt it.*

Giant tree roots curled from the ground like fat boa constrictors. In one marshy place, where walking meant balancing on boards, a small spring bubbled clean water. After swimming, wading, splashing in the salty bay, when they arrived at this spring, they cupped their hands, dipped into the icy, sweet fresh water, and washed their faces.

After the spring, light began to shine into the forest as trees grew further apart. And soon, only one huge tree stood, with one great low limb almost touching the ground: an old oak. Walking past the oak, they found a few apple trees with small bug-bitten apples: hard, round, and unappealing.

After the apple trees came the open field filled with tall grass where Queen Anne's lace and daisies grew in clumps. Max picked two daisies for his mom.

Charles tried to pick a few stalks of Queen Anne's lace, but instead pulled them up by their roots. He was horrified and wondered what to do. Then he remembered the trowel in his pack. He took it out and sawed the blade across the tough stems until they were cut through, then poured water from his bottle into the hole and pushed the roots back in the disturbed earth. He hoped they would reroot. He poured more water and patted the ground around them. Charles rubbed his dirty hands on the silky grass and used the grass to wipe his trowel clean before he put it away. He carried his two flowers as if they were the most precious treasure he'd ever held.

When everyone had assembled at the truck, each had a treasure. Fred had found a well-worked stone, perhaps the beginning of an arrowhead. Zipper displayed a piece of birch bark she curled around her little finger. Max had a stick in the shape of a tiny snake: one end like a mouth was open with a splinter sticking out like a tongue. Pat had a tiny bird's skull bleached white; it had died a long time ago. Charles showed the Queen Anne's lace. All were treasures. Pat had an empty shoe box in the back of his truck. Each discovery was carefully placed there.

Chapter 6
Ice Cream First, Then The Periwinkle Shop

"Iigh noon on August 12:
A truck and van arrive,
The town of Deer Isle
  Invaded by Marylanders.
  No other vehicles on road.
  No people in sight.
  Doors and windows
  of buildings closed
  but lights are on,
  air conditioners hum.
  Truck and van parallel park
  beside sidewalk.
  Drivers slip clutches into park,
  set emergency brakes.
  The invasion includes
  a passenger from
  one island."

Max's imagination saw the unfolding action as a script for a movie, video, or TV reality drama. *Slowly pan camera down a quiet street. Pause for glimpses of distant bay waters twinkling between shops. Zoom in: first on truck, then on van. Discover both are filled to capacity with shapes and sizes . . . show only shadows of bodies, no faces, count 5 seconds, time for viewer to notice crowded vehicle interiors vs. outside emptiness. Begin dramatic music, something classical? No lyrics . . . . (Oh yeah! the haunting theme from an old TV series, "The Twilight Zone." That's it. Of course.)* Max kept his thoughts to himself but grinned.

No one noticed Max's smile because Charles was filling the truck with the noise of his questions:

"What's this place?" He was looking at the row of two-story wooden buildings built right up to the wide sidewalk along the street. In the gaps between each building, one could see the bay glittering. "I don't see anyone or anything happening. Is this a movie set for a ghost town?"

Shivers ran through Max: *Copy that: ghost town idea for film.*

"Nope," said Pat. "It's a real place. It's even a real town where you can have Maine Black Bear, Moose Tracks, or a Black Fly."

"What?"

"Those are ice cream flavors. See? Over there is an old-fashioned ice cream parlor. There are other flavors for those less bold. Twists, vanilla, strawberry, chocolate, or you could go for a Blue Smurf," Fred said. He'd taken out his camera. With the zoom lens, he was reading flavors on a small sign hung beside the door. "There's no carry-out window. It has no drive-through window. You're forced to get out and go inside."

Meanwhile, inside both truck and van, bodies in all sizes, shapes, dress, and age were uncurling from riding positions, sliding doors opened and they bounced free from enclosures.

"An ice cream shop. Perfect, we'll have dessert first," said Zipper's Aunt Popee. "Life is always best when the last comes first."

In the town, they found outside doors were shut but not locked, and some windows left open. Pat opened the door to the little sweets shop and they all meandered in: tall, short, half -asleep older teens, wide-awake toddler, hungry preteens, eager men, and decision-making women.

Behind the counter a cheerful-looking older woman with short-cropped, wispy brown hair, reading glasses hugging her nose between long eyelashes and tips of nostrils, looked up from the local weekly paper she'd been reading. She whistled at the size of the group. Immediately, she cheerfully began half humming, half singing: "Enter the young . . . . hmmm. Here they come. Here they Come. Here they come, yeah."

"That's a song by a group called The Association," Zipper's Aunt Popee said to Max. "They were at the top on pop charts when Pat, Fred, and I were teens." Singing and humming when words escaped their memories, Pat, Mom, and Fred continued the song the woman behind the counter had begun:

Pat sang, "Some are walking,"

Fred, pointing to little Carrie, "Some are riding,"

All adults in unison: "Here they come, yeah."

What followed was adult laughter and moans, groans, smiles, and smirks from the younger people in the group.

"Well, welcome, folks. Name's Finch, like the bird, but I don't have lovely golden feathers. Then again I'm brown like a mama finch, so I guess it works. Nice to have someone come in who knows songs from my era, an oldie but goodie. Did I just say *oldie?* Ugh, no way. What can I get you folks today?"

"Ice cream! We're going to live backwards: have dessert before a picnic lunch and swim at The Lily Pond. Do you think we're living too dangerously, Finch? Oh, and by the way, I'm Popee."

"Popee? Love it! Always important to have dessert first; you sound like my kind of people," said Finch. "Here's a list of all our special Maine flavors. They arrived here today. Just made this morning, or so I was told! We also have twists. The Twist of The Day is black raspberry with chocolate. It may sound strange but it tastes, oh my goodness, wicked good."

Desserts chosen and served, dished or scooped, the assorted sizes and ages moved to a back deck where they could look out at the bay while enjoying their sweet treats. Carrie sat on Fred's lap. Mom sat beside them with Twist of the Day in a cup for Carrie, who licked the spoon coated with tasty ice cream. Fred managed his own cone of Moose Tracks. Pat was the only one to dare Black Fly, which was actually vanilla with chocolate chips (black flies) and swirls of raspberry to represent what a black fly bite might do to a person. Maine Black Bear was the favorite and right behind it, the less original but tasty vanilla and/or chocolate twist with colored sprinkles. T. L. Toni selected a diet soda and left the deck to window-shop in the tiny stores. Ralph ate his two-scoop cone too quickly to have enjoyed its taste and was lucky to have escaped getting a brain freeze. As soon as possible, he finished and went to join Toni.

"Poor Ralph, life ruled by a girl," Charles said.

Pat and Fred attempted not to laugh. Mom carefully corrected Charles, "Now, Charles, that's not a nice thing to say."

Max looked at Zipper and in a whisper, hopefully not heard by the adults, said, "T. L. Toni's been ruling Ralph's life ever since they met in sixth grade."

"Did Ralph and Toni graduate from high school this year?" Zipper asked.

"Yes," said Max.

"And college?"

"Toni's staying local, attending a community college in Baltimore. Ralph is off to college in Boston." Max said.

"Well, distance will either make the heart grow fonder or will give them the space they need to grow as they ought," Zipper said. She stood looking out at the bay, licking what was left of her chocolate-caramel sea salt cone. Max turned so he could watch the bay. He nibbled the end of his waffle cone and let the sweet melted ice cream drip onto his tongue. When Zipper looked his way, she raised an eyebrow, and Max said, "Hey, I'm not twelve until ten o'clock so I'll let this be one of my last eleven-year-old childish delights."

"Don't worry, Max," Zipper said. "You can keep acting like a little boy and eating ice cream any way you want; it's obvious you're way older than twelve, in a good way."

Most everyone was finished and washing sticky hands using some of Carrie's Wet Ones when Ralph returned to the deck to check in.

"Neat store across the road, the Periwinkle Shop: penny candy, postcards, T-shirts, homemade stuff, and a few famous books autographed by locals. I think you'll enjoy it. I'm going back there now. Right across from here," he pointed and left.

"Well, let's check it out," said Fred. "An autographed book by a famous local writer could someday be quite a treasure."

"Hmm, penny candy, one of my favorites," said Charles.

The Periwinkle Shop was all Ralph had advertised and more. Books by local authors included those by Robert McCloskey and Barbara Anne Cooney. Pat and Popee, Fred and Mom bought four classic children's books each. Mom and Fred picked *Make Way for Ducklings, Blueberries for Sal, A Time to Wonder,* and *Miss Rumphias.* Pat and Popee's choices were: *One Morning in Maine, A Time to Wonder, Miss Rumphias,* and *When the Sky is Like Lace* (by Elinor Lander Horwitz).

"Zip, is there any book you'd like? Consider it a belated birthday present from your Aunt Popee and me?" Pat asked.

96

"Well, hmm. I have all the books by Mr. McCloskey; he's someone I go and visit some Sundays. But, ah, maybe the book *When the Sky Is Like Lace*. I think I would like to own that one, if you really don't mind?"

"It would be our pleasure," said her aunt.

"You really know Mr. McCloskey?" Max asked. "What's he like?"

"He has the kindest smile and the bluest eyes; a really nice man. I know one of his daughters, too. You should visit him or his daughter sometime," Zipper said.

Meanwhile, Charles sat on the floor under the counter. In front of him were thirty jars of penny candy. The shop owner, Miss N., had given him a bag to fill. 'Will *all* that I want plus some to share fit in this bag?' Charles pondered. He took out strips of candy dots, scoops of Mary Janes, Swedish Fish, Turkish Taffy, licorice sticks, and last but not least, a hand filled with some hot, spicy cinnamon Fire Balls. *What a feast!*

Miss N. rang up all their purchases on an old-fashioned cash register.

"What a work of art," Fred said, admiring the polished nickel engraved sides of the old machine. "And look at those keys? Wow!" It was a museum piece used by Miss N. in the store.

"I know it may seem foolish. It should be locked away, but I think the store and I would lose specialness if it wasn't here. Silly ol' me, I guess," she laughed. "It just wouldn't seem like The Periwinkle Shop anymore if it didn't sit here on this counter. It was passed down in my family one generation to another. It's been here with me in the shop ever since the first day I unlocked the door, opened for business . . . . that was, well, before you children were born. I opened it one summer in the mid-1960s. It's been my joy to open it every summer since."

When the time came, they all waved good bye to Miss. R. and scurried across the empty road to van and truck.

"We'll come back again, before our vacation ends, won't we, Mom?" Charles asked.

"My goodness, you didn't get enough penny candy?" Fred asked.

"Oh, probably I'll need another bag . . . I mean we'll need another bag. I'm sharing. Even if I had enough candy, I'd still like to go back and visit with Miss N.," Charles said.

"Me, too," said Max.

"I love my visits with her," said Zipper.

"Looks like it's unanimous, Fred," said Pat.

"Yep. Sure, why not. But now it's to the pond!"

"Finally!" said Ralph.

Chapter 7
Swimming in a Lily Pond? Are You Sure?

"Look for the sign *Path to the Pond*," Pat said as they drove into the parking lot of a senior housing complex. This was the place they'd been told to go by locals who trusted them. It was a special pond. Only a few "people from away" were told how to find it: "You'll find a sign: *Path to the Pond*—take it," they had said.

"Not to worry, Uncle Pat, I know the way. Park over there where there's shade," Zipper directed him.

"I should have known to ask you, Zip," Pat said, pulling the truck into the shady parking slot. "Been here lots?"

"Yep, hot summers, days at a time as long as the weather allows," Zipper said.

Fred parked the van behind Pat.

All out.

"Helping line starts here," said Mom. "We've lots to carry in and need everyone's help (except Carrie)."

Coolers, raft, kayaks, paddles, foam noodles; bags filled with blankets, towels; two bags of food: sliced bakery bread, locally made honey, jams and jellies, and Maine's favorite marshmallow sandwich treat: Fluff with healthy-choice fresh-ground peanut butter; fishing rods, tackle boxes, landing nets, and rubber buckets for the fish caught; folding chairs; walker, water, and beach toys for Carrie.

"Oh, boy, you all, this is the most stuff I've seen any group haul into the pond," said Zipper.

"It's a bit of a walk. Nobody try to be Mr. or Ms. Tough and carry too much," said Mom.

"All pitch in and help," said Fred.

And they did.

The Path to the Pond twisted through a woods of birch, apple, maples, young and massively old pines, and fir trees. For a short while, it opened into fields where they were pleased to find ripe wild blueberries waiting to be picked. It was a 10-minute walk but seemed longer to all except Zipper. Soon the deep blue of the pond could be seen, then a grassy lawn. They had arrived.

"Find a good place. Shade and sun. Sun for those who wish to sunbathe; shade for others," Mom said. "It's deserted here today. Why's that?"

"Well, it is 1:00 p.m. on a Monday, the 12th of August. For local children and teens, camps are still in session. For Southern summer guests with children, many have gone back home to prepare for school opening. And then maybe rumor has gotten out—we were coming," Pat joked.

They all laughed, even Toni and Ralph.

"Yep, lots of college kids had to go back this week for orientation and all that stuff. Toni and I are lucky. Our colleges don't start until after Labor Day Weekend."

"Like our school," said Charles.

"They don't want to see us until the Wednesday after Labor Day. They want the teachers to have in-service days to prepare themselves . . . . for us," Max said.

More laughter.

"It's beautiful here. Look how calm the water is.... Smooth as—oh, I know it's a cliché, but truly look, it's smooth as smooth can be. Let's stop standing around. Let's go in and enjoy it!" said Mom.

"Last one in is a goose egg," yelled Charles, stripping down to his bathing suit.

Max and Zipper did the same. All three sprinted into the silent, smooth surface of the pond.

100

"Where do we change? Where is the bathroom?" Toni asked.

"No changing rooms or bathrooms or outhouses here," Mom said. "I'm afraid it's roughing it, Toni."

"Those dense high trees and reeds are where I'm going to change," said Popee.

"As far as a bathroom, Popee or I will stand guard when you need to do what you need to do in those tall bushes," said Mom. "I have my suit on under my clothes so I'll stay here like the boys did and peel off a few layers. And Carrie gets to swim in a diaper."

"Pat and I also have suits on under our shorts . . . we've already had a splash in the bay. I'm anxious to enjoy warm and clean pond water," said Fred.

Ralph looked sheepish. "Sorry, Toni, I should have warned you there would be days like today. "

"Oh, it's okay. I'm actually wearing my bathing suit on under my shorts and T, too," Toni said. She went to the area where her towel, suntan lotion, and other personals were and began to strip down to her suit.

Mom's reaction: "Oh, my," she said to Popee, "I believe Toni's beginning to grow up or at least beginning to buy into the Maine experience."

"Maybe, a bit of both and it is good to see."

"The water is amazing! You need to come in!" Charles yelled. He swam after Max and Zipper.

"Here, Charles. Look how tall I am now!" Zipper said. She'd found what was known as "the rock pile."

"I'm checking it out," said Max, diving down. Five feet deep, deeper, the water was clear and so clean, he could see the bottom. Diving down, he examined the place where teens had piled rocks, building a pile high and wide enough for two medium-size youth to stand on side by side. He did a headstand, flipped back, and surfaced.

"Saw your feet just now," said Charles.

"The water is crystal-clear, Charles. Not muddy at all. You should try swimming underwater," Max told him.

"That's my plan. I've a bit of spying to do. Will report back what's happening with Ralph and T.L.," Charles said. He dove down and swam underwater until he was on the far left side of the pond's bank.

On that side, the pond bottom was soft and squishy, not welcoming to one who liked hard bottom and clear water, but Charles wanted to be hidden and here he was, by high, blue flowering plants known as pickerel weeds. He'd heard Popee name them to Mom when they first arrived. Pat had added, "Good weeds. Their seeds help feed wild ducks."

In the place where Charles hid, white water lilies with egg-yellow centers were growing in tight clusters. Their roots were long and stringlike; near the pond's bank, they were an unruly mass, something to stay away from or you might get your legs tangled and you could be tripped.

Charles's hiding place was near but not in "Frog Town," where every spring little children liked to net tadpoles and people his age tried their skill at hand-catching fast adult amphibians. But today, no one else was anywhere near Frog Town, which made spying and listening easier. Charles kept underwater, from bottom lip down, only nose, cheeks, ears, and soggy hair were out. But using reeds and mud, he was camouflaged and blended in with weedy growth and dark shadows. He thought of himself as "The Unseen."

From his hiding spot, Charles watched family and friends and heard their conversations coming from the grassy lawn less than thirty feet away. Later, this is what he reported back to Max and Zipper:

"Want to go for a swim?" Ralph asked T. L. Toni. "Or maybe take the kayak out...."

"Sounds like a good idea, Toni," Popee said. "Go on, you two take the kayak for a paddle. Zipper is over there on the Rock Pile. She'll point out the spot where older teens go. We'll keep the rest from following," Under her baggy clothes, she wore a black bathing suit. She held Carrie while Mom slipped off shorts and shirt and both began to laugh. They were wearing identical black bathing suits. Not planned. "A coincidence," Mom said. "It's the style and color all the best-dressed women are wearing this year." They laughed.

Ralph asked T.L. Toni, "Want to kayak? It's a two-seater. You get tired, I can manage the paddling."

Then *Big Surprise!* T. L. Toni said, "Sure." She slipped out of her shorts and removed her chic, Valley Girl best lacy, white cotton blouse. Under it, she wasn't wearing much, an itty-bitty black bikini. But she asked, "Do you have life jackets?"

"In the kayak. We'll launch right from this beach," Ralph said.

"Let's do it," said Toni.

And so they did.

Toni helped Ralph push the kayak across the grass to the bank and into the water. He held it steady while she got in. He followed, sliding in like a natural. Then both began paddling about, headed into the deepest part of the pond. Mom said, "I think she's beginning to fit in."

Aunt Popee said, "A matter of maturing. . . . Being away from the peer pressure I think is good for her. Boys and girls raised in the 'burbs of major cities, surrounded by malls, not

103

parks or other ways to recreate in nature, are always on this
'look at me, do this, must fit in pressure' and they miss (as she
has missed) the beauty of down time, which we all need.
Kayaking with Ralph is an excellent idea."

Then Charles heard Mom agree. She said, "Hopefully,
the entire vacation will be full of adventures and an entrance
into nature and restful for all of us."

Aunt Popee said, "It's good having Zipper here today.
She shows us all what living on a Maine island is like."

That's when Charles decided to rejoin Max and Zipper.
"I figured I better wash off the mud and join you two here on
this rock pile, otherwise Ralph might wonder where I was,"
Charles said. "I dove down and crab-walked with my hands
on the bottom, halfway here to these rocks. Geez, pond mud
is disgusting. Glad to be back in clean water."

Charles did a feet-in-air flip before surfacing beside the
kayak. He was there just in time to hear Zipper give Ralph
and T. L. Toni directions.

"Paddle straight out. When you're in the middle of the
pond, look left, you can't miss seeing a huge rock ledge.
Usually someone is swinging out on the Tarzan swing. But if
you do it, swing waa-aay far out. If you don't, you could get
scratched and hurt by sharp rocks," Zipper warned.

"Okay, thanks, Zipper, see you later," said Ralph.

"Thanks!" said T. L. Toni.

Max, Charles, and Zipper watched the two teens paddle
in sync up the middle of the pond. When they were out of
earshot, Charles made his report about all he had overheard.

"T. L. Toni is paddling better than I ever thought she
could," Max said. "The kayak's going straight and isn't acting
tippy."

"Maybe she's not the Valley Girl you thought she was," Zipper said. She shallow-dove off the rock pile to the deeper side of the pond. "The rock pile is all yours, Charles," she said. "I'm going for a swim: try for body shots in and out of water. Max, are you going for a swim?"

"Sure. In a minute," Max turned to Charles. "Good report, 'Unseen'. Are you going to swim?"

"Are you kidding? Of course. I don't want to get rusty. I can butterfly here and no one will be watching, except maybe Zipper and you. I doubt I'll go where T. L and Ralph are. If I do, I'll zip back as fast I can away from them."

"Good, good. Maybe you and Zipper can race. You know me. I like to swim lazy," Max said.

"Got you covered." Charles shifted into crawl mode. He began swiftly swimming up center pond where the path was wide and clear of the green lily pads and the white and yellow blooms that grew on each side of the water.

Max rolled onto his back. He rocked, floating on the wake Charles had made. Then, as the water settled, he experienced the glorious feeling of being held on the surface, as if hundreds of tiny hands with cushioned palms were making a soft bed for him to rest on. *Grandpa gifted me big-time when he taught me how to float,* Max thought.

A few minutes later he tilted his head forward. He could see Mom and Aunt Popee watching Carrie play on the sandy beach with her bag of beach toys. He listened to her baby laughs ringing, echoing around the pond. He saw how happy Carrie made Mom and Aunt Popee. Well, no surprise, she made everybody happy, though he and Charles were really not into getting silly over babies. Still, Carrie had been their interesting study since the moment they met her, 30 minutes after her birth. As she got older, she'd begun to be a "person" they both liked.

Max was happy Mom and Fred had a baby together to share. *Fred never made Charles, Ralph, or me feel different. We're all his kids. I hear ugly stuff around school about parents splitting up, getting remarried, new parents never, ever treating them like their own kid. I can't understand people who'd act like that. I'm sure glad Fred and Mom never did.*

On the beach he heard more noise and saw that the other kayak had been launched. He saw Fred and Pat snapping on life jackets.

All's well, Max thought. He let his head rest back on the water and stared at his ten toes. When he wiggled them, they made little rings on the calm surface. *Perhaps I was a canoe or kayak in a former life. No, impossible, they're made from wood or plastics or something. Then what could I have been? Oh, okay, I know, maybe a loon. Yes, a loon is more me than goose, duck, seagull, or cormorant.* He stared up at the blue sky. He relaxed.

In a few moments, Fred and Pat went by in the kayak. "Where's Charles and Zipper?" Pat asked.

"Oh, way ahead, I guess, maybe having a race. You know how much Charles loves competitive swimming."

"He sure does! His bedroom walls are covered in ribbons and trophies won in swim meets. Walking in there feels like walking into a display cabinet," Fred said. He was beaming.

Max knew Fred and Mom were happy that Charles was a great swimmer. If his head had always been in some book, others might have accused him of being a nerd. But in school and at meets everywhere, everybody knew: Charles *was* a great swimmer. And to make it sweeter, Charles loved swimming. Max knew Charles's success as a swimmer would help him fit in better when he got older. To be a sports winner in middle and high school was really important.

Fred and Pat paddled away and Max was alone again.

No one was near.

Now he was in the quiet water, alone as he had not been all day since waking at 3:30 a.m. . . . . more alone than walking at the Preserve where The Cemetery was, because there he knew someone was ahead and someone was following him. But here, floating on the pond's water, Max let his mind wander, let random thoughts wiggle through his imagination; new ideas popped from nowhere. Here, at this moment, floating, being almost one with pond water, he remembered the strange note left by the blueberry pie. What could it mean? Did it mean anything? Was its meaning already over? Was its meaning beginning? Or what?

> "It will happen at some time
> Be it while the sun is bright
> Or on a starry night."

Max thought of all the things that had happened since 3:30 a.m.:

> crows and seagulls at first light;
> seeing Zipper for the first time;
> watching sunrise on the beach;
> all the creatures she'd introduced them to in the tidal pools;
> how magical the day seemed;
> a periwinkle coming out of its shell,
> when Charles hummed sea tunes to it;
> the starfish/sea star he held;
> hermit crabs skittering.

the beauty of the place Pat called Paradise;

hiking the blue blaze trail;

watching horrified as an eagle tore apart a dead seagull,

and the final win by all those gulls.

The Cemetery and the words on the stone he'd rubbed;

how it was the same gravestone Zipper placed flowers on;

where she'd stayed the longest.

Max had read the message on that stone. It filled him with curiosity and wonder. He wondered if the others had found messages on the stones they'd rubbed as powerful as the one he'd found. He'd memorized the poem.

Now, floating on the glassy still of The Lily Pond, his ears in the water below the surface, all he heard was water and sounds of his body. He said the words from the gravestone over and over to himself:

"Dearest Anna gone from life

Spirit freed from flesh, now dust,

I promise our infant daughter, Zepporah,

Shall know you through memories I'll share.

God's way man does not understand,

But our love lives.

This place of woodlands and sea

Will always surround what it once meant

To be, you and me.   Always my love, John

Zepporah—Zipper's real name and the name of Moses' wife who traveled through a wilderness. All day, Max had felt like he was being drawn by Zipper to journey further and further away from the world he'd known before, into something different.

Today, what an adventure and . . . there's something yet to happen. I feel like every hour is a stepping stone leading me (us to a place we've never been before and afterwards we'll be changed forever. When? Who exactly is Zipper? What will happen? How will things spin, creating . . .

Whoosh! Zipper appeared like an explosion near his feet, bursting out of the water, then diving back in. She took hold of his toes and began spinning him. "Whaaa?"

"Floating like an island, Max? Come on, time to swim." She disappeared.

Next he felt her under him, pushing against his shoulders, and this made his body fold in half. He was forced to roll over, change position in the water, go from his state of being lost in imagination into actively swimming. He began the side stroke, then breast stroke. Zipper continued swimming around him, diving under the water, surfacing, down under, and then surfacing again. Circling and encouraging Max to swim.

"Where to?" he sputtered.

"Back to the beach, silly," Zipper said. "Your mom and Aunt Popee have been calling for three or four minutes. It's time to eat . . . again. Come on," she said.

"Where's Charles?"

"See those whitewater waves between the Tarzan swing and us? That's Charles. He's practicing his butterfly stroke."

Max stopped, turned, treading water as he looked back. He saw a moving figure pushing out, dashing down, then raising up, more dolphin than human swimmer. "No, really? I've never seen him move so fast. Wow, if he keeps that speed and takes it home, he'll be medaling right and left."

"Yes, he's beginning to understand the rhythms and ways . . . how his body moves wavelike. To do the butterfly stroke well, he must move his body in the same way aquatic creatures do," Zipper said. She slid in circles around Max, her hair swirling about her body, another kind of living wave.

"You cued him in, I bet."

"He was ready. He knew how. I just told him: 'Believe in you and work with the water.' I showed him some breathing tricks: inhale through his mouth, exhale mouth or nose, doesn't matter. And maybe only breathe in every three strokes, breathe out whenever it's most comfortable. Better ways to breathe and maintain speed or increase it and ways to use his hands. Hands are very important. He got it right away and he's really polishing his style."

"He sure is."

Together they headed to shore, Zipper circling him like some sleek water creature. Like what . . . . Like the big brown-eyed harbor seals he'd seen appear, disappear, scoot, dive, roll on their backs, gracefully playing in the water. Zipper—with her long dark hair surrounding her and her graceful dives, dashes, scoots, underwater wavy moves—reminded Max of the mysterious seals he'd always loved to watch in Wild Water Wild Creature Park or other nature programs. But unlike harbor seals, when on land, she continued to be graceful.

It was a simple lunch eaten in rounds as kayakers and swimmers returned to shore: a meal of breads, jams, jellies, Marshmallow Fluff, and watermelon slices.

"A simple light lunch; dinner in a few hours and you must save room," Mom said.

After everyone had eaten, it was free time again: time to rest, nap, swim, sunbathe, read, write, sketch, take

110

photographs, play with frogs down near the reeds, make a sand castle, walk the trail around The Lily Pond to the Tarzan swing, or send a fly line after the little sunfish, brook trout, and bass. There were many choices during free time.

5:00 p.m. time to clean up, pack, and haul out all they'd hauled in. The walk to the parking lot seemed only a few moments, the drive to the cottages less than 10 minutes.

Chapter 8
Dinner at Eaton's Lobster Pool

"H ome" at the cottages, Mom announced: "Please take showers. Wash off the pond. We'll leave here at 6:15. As far as dress code," she said, "Eaton's Lobster Pool is not a place you need to be dressed fancy for."

"In fact, if your jeans and T-shirt are a few days old, it's okay. Why? Because no matter what seafood dish you might order, you'll probably be wearing some of it before you finish eating. This is especially true for lobster. Even if you order something less messy, there's a good chance someone nearby will order lobster and when they crack open a claw or rip the body section from the tail, many times lobster juices fly everywhere. Eating a whole lobster is a messy job," Pat said.

"If you order a Maine red hot dog. . . . Yes, you heard me, the skins are red, or if you chicken out with buffalo wings and drumsticks, hamburger or steak, even if you're sitting alone down on the beach, you might stay clean, except for the sand and mud. And anyway, I ask you, very seriously, who wants to order meat when going to Eaton's Lobster Pool?" asked Aunt Popee.

Showered, dressed in the same jeans and clean, rumpled T-shirts, Charles and Max were the first ones ready to go. Finding Scrabble on a shelf with puzzles and games, they decided to play outside on the porch while they waited for the others. They set up the board on a small deck table and pulled up two chairs.

Three rounds into the game, Zipper was the next person to emerge. Her long wet hair was a single braid, centered and falling down her back. She wore bibbed overalls, the same yellowed waffle-weave shirt, her bare feet stuck into hiking shoes. The oversized brown sweater was tied around her middle.

"Want to join us in a game of Scrabble?" Max asked. He was being friendly. He also wanted a restart as the letters on his tiles were horrible and Charles had been racking up big points ever since round one.

"Yes. Great! I like Scrabble lots," Zipper said. Zipper found a chair and pulled it up. Charles frowned as he placed all of his tiles with the others in the little blue velvet bag. Max smiled ear to ear as he added his. *A new game, yeah,* he thought.

Twenty minutes of wordsmithing, points taken, scores added and announced, Charles shrewdly placed the highest-valued tiles on the highest-scoring squares.

"Oh, yes!"

"Score!"

"Are you sure that's a real word? I call for proof. Where's the dictionary?" Then they heard a noise.

T.L. Toni pushed open the screen door and walked onto the deck. She swung a silver purse strap in one hand and *Vogue* magazine in the other. She looked around then sat in the porch swing. She was wearing an L.L. Bean summer dress and brand-new white sandals. *Not good,* Max thought.

Moments later Max saw Mom looking through the screen door. She motioned for him to come in.

"Be back in a minute. Don't look at my tiles," he told Charles. Zipper he trusted.

Inside, Mom said, "Max, do me a favor. Check all the storage places here. See if you can find any spot remover for laundry use. If not, please go over and ask Aunt Popee if she has some I can borrow. I'm getting ready before we leave in case I'm cleaning Toni's clothes and shoes after a dinner at Eaton's."

"I'm on it, Mom." Max said. He searched and within minutes found a plastic bottle: "Get Out, Get Out, You Ugly Spot, You!" was hidden on a back shelf in the laundry room cabinet of their cottage. He gave it to Mom.

"Thanks, sweetie," she said, giving him a kiss on the top of his combed, need-a-haircut head. "Now go back to your game."

Max went back to the table. Charles was winning. No surprise.

Promptly at 6:15, everyone was ready, sitting in both vehicles, engines humming.

Emergency brakes clicked down, clutch in, off they went with Pat driving his truck, leading the way. This time it was a right onto Route 15, head toward The Bridge, but just before it, fast left, then another near the entrance to a little white church.

The road was a sloping, crooked, unmarked sandy lane. It dipped down, bounced up, curved to the right around flowering beach roses; it narrowed to the width of a driveway, passed by an old gray-shingled house with gray picket fence and the garden overflowing into the drive lane was a mass of bright flowers: red and orange geraniums, purple asters, assorted day lilies. Beside this house, old-style lobster traps, made of wood and rope were stacked and marked for sale.

"Tourist traps," smirked Pat. He made another left, a right, then down another unmarked sandy lane, no wider than a driveway.

"Are you sure this is correct, Pat?" asked Charles.

"Oh, yeah. You need to be clued in on how to find some of these places. Maine Philosophy 101: 'If you don't know how to get somewhere, you're not supposed to be there.' That's just how it is in parts of Down East Maine." He laughed. "Keep the riffraff out." He slowed the truck as he pulled into a graveled parking lot where ten cars, in assorted conditions from waxed shiny to rusted-out, different makes, years, license plates from different states, were parked. "Here we are," Pat said.

Fred eased the van in and parked beside the truck.

All climbed over and out.

Before them, tall grass grew two feet high, waving in the slight sea breeze. Beyond the grasses was the muddy beach. They could smell the sweet-harsh raw, definitely *real* smell of bracken at low tide.

"Where's the restaurant?" T. L. Toni asked, looking all around then back to Pat.

"We're at it . . . or rather on its grounds. Look, over there? See the little path off to the right? Take it. In a few minutes, you'll see. No joke, we're here."

"How about follow our leader?" Fred suggested.

"Good idea," said Pat. "Follow me. . . . Oh, any of you older folk remember this from John Denver's 1970 album *Take Me to Tomorrow*? Pat began singing and humming forgotten lyrics as he led them down a sandy path, wide enough for one person at a time. Fred, Popee, and Mom began to hum and sing with him.

By the last "follow me," they were steps away from a weather-worn gray, one- story building. In front were picnic tables, which began in the field and went down to the shore. A rusty screen door to be pushed open. Next to it sat a cat patiently waiting, seeking a chance to sneak in. Beside the door, a white painted sign with faded words read: *Welcome.*

Open Monday-Saturday 11:00-8:30 p.m. Closed Sundays, so we can have a day of rest.

Pat pushed the screen door in and held it: cat first, then the group all squeezed into a small lobby. "Stand to your right, hug the wall; in other words, stay as close to the wall as you can," Pat said.

When everyone was in, Pat entered, letting the screen door gently close. On a front wall was a big white sign that read: *Market Price of the Day* and listed below were:

> *Soft shell clams*   *by the pound*
> *Blue mussels*   *bag or pound*
> *Oysters*   *by pound or dozen, shucked, bagged*
>   *raw in shell ready to go*
> *Haddock, whole, sandwich . . . or by pound to "travel"*
> *Lobster 1, 1 ¼, 1 ½, 1 ¾ or twin lobster dinner.*
> *One hot dog, two hot dogs with home-style baked beans*
> *Chicken wings (Buffalo style), legs or breasts*
> *All dinners include chips, barrel dill pickle, cold slaw/*
> *potato salad, pie (ice cream sundaes extra)*

Under this sign was a large wooden cooler filled with seawater and bagged ice. Here they saw bags of mussels and oysters, containers filled with shucked oysters, and beside them, on plastic sheets, fillets of haddock. Beside the fish area were two tall, red, old-fashioned Coca-Cola coolers with "cap popper" on their sides. A small sign read: *Open for drinks, please close tight when you get one.*

"First, grab your soda, then go over there. When all of us have our drinks, we'll flag someone and tell them we'll be dining here tonight," Pat said.

All found drinks and went like lambs to Pat.

They were grouped near what had once been a lectern from a church. Now it was painted purple and pink, with the wooden cross down the middle painted gold. "All things are recycled here," Pat said.

Moments later, the hostess/waitress appeared. She was wearing a tight, low-cut, pink tank top, cut-off jeans, and pink flip-flops. "Hey, name's Hattie. I'll be your server today."

Hattie was deeply tanned. Her shaggy long hair was a rosy natural blond streaked with gray. She was about fifty (so the group guessed later), her voice raspy from too many cigarettes, body a bit beefy. She had a tattoo of a ruby-throated red-and-green male hummingbird on her left arm, a magenta flower on her right. Woven colorful bracelets looped both her wrists, another on her left ankle. Two gold rings on two of her pink-painted toes.

"What's her name?" Charles whispered to Max.

"Hattie," Max whispered back. "I guess it must have been a popular name a long time ago." To himself he thought, *We keep meeting people named Hattie, in Maryland and in Maine, on letters, tombstones, and now our waitstaff person.*

"My, my, you *are* quite a big group! Lucky us!" Hattie said. "Let's see. I count nine. Oh, I see one more. Will she need a need a high chair?"

"Yes. Thanks, a high chair would be great," said Mom. "What a relief no one has to hold Carrie while eating lobsters," she whispered to Fred, who was carrying the squirmy one-year-old.

"Okay, follow me. There's seating with a good view near the windows . . . all the way in the back."

"Perfect," said Pat.

"I figure you want inside, right? It's beginning to get a bit chilly. Sea breeze startin' to kick in."

"Warm is good," Fred said.

They followed Hattie over creaky, uneven plywood floors. It was an uninsulated building; nails from outside wooden planks came through the plywood walls. No Sheetrock or paint. Everywhere was the natural beauty of knotty pine.

Following Hattie, they easily read what was stamped on her work shirt: *Eaton's Lobster Pool. No Swimmin' Fools nor Foolin' Allowed.* Pictured were cartoons of lobsters, clams, mussels, and fish as cooks, chefs, waitresses, and waiters; a black cauldron sat on bright red flames, a cowboy hat floated on the boiling brine.

They passed one small group in L.L. Bean Maine summer attire, but all other customers were dressed as if they'd arrived from working outside: gardening, carpentry, on boats, some were still wet from swims or showers. Some people looked like artists with all shades of paint chips splotched on shirts and jeans, while others scribbled words on yellow tablets. Beside soda, those over 21 were allowed BYOB beer or wine in brown bags. Eaton's would provide icy pitchers for beer or plastic-stemmed wine glasses. Most people looked like they belonged; many had been customers for years.

Walking the long walk to their picnic table, Max noticed names written in crayon and ballpoint on bare pine walls: colorful crayoned initials or *Molly loves you always Mort,*" "Hey, you *****. *You said this was a good time date, not a final good-bye suppah', you **** creep.*"

Hattie noticed Max reading the walls and said, "If you try and read all the messages, we'll be wallowing our way to your table for hours. Enjoy reading the walls once you're seated and waitin' for your dinnah or when you're chewin' it up."

118

She stopped and began flipping menus onto three picnic tables pushed together with a wooden high chair for Carrie at one end. They worked their way into a formation that would be a good fit, and when all were comfortable, they sat.

"You already have your drinks. Read over the menu and I'll be back by the count of 29 (seconds, that is)." And she was gone, sweeping up trash, flatware, and tips from empty tables as she passed.

In front of them the restaurant was mostly glass with a view of the water . . . at low tide. Out on the mud, people were raking for clams, filling little wooden baskets. Pat answered the unspoken question. "Yes, clams, but not to worry, Eaton's has those muddy guys bathed and ready when you order them. Or the cherrystones are fixed on the half shell. Everything is grit- and mud-free."

They quickly scanned the menu but most knew what they wanted and when 28 ½ seconds had passed (Charles was timing on his watch), Hattie was back.

"Okay, how's my time, young fella?"

"You're ½ second early," Charles said, smiling.

"Need another ½ second?" she laughed.

"Nope," said Pat. "We're ready."

"Well, all righty then. Let me get your orders in. Your appetizers will be out quick. You can be nibbling on something while waiting for the rest. Appetizers featured tonight: fresh greens from a farm near Sedgwick, just across The Bridge, tomatoes are grown right here. We have bread from the gal up the road. She told me she pulled it out of her ovens about 6:00 p.m. Let's see, you have a choice: plain, blueberry (mighty fine), molasses, whole wheat, and corn muffins . . . . or, if you'd like, I can bring a couple of baskets with assorted . . . what's your pleasure?"

"Three baskets of assorted," Pat said. "And your homemade butter."

"You've been here before. I remember you and you," she said, pointing to Aunt Popee. "And you, well, you live on Isle au Haut, don't you?" she asked Zipper.

"Yep," said Zipper. "And these folks are family and friends who are like family."

"Well, then, you'll get my best service," Hattie said with a "down home" grin. "Anything else to chew on? We have some good locally grown raw carrots and celery with ranch or a homemade lemon and cream horseradish for dipping."

"Yes!" said Mom and Popee together. They laughed.

"We'll take two orders of the raw veggies, one with ranch and one with homemade," Popee said. She looked at Mom and whispered, "It's yummy."

"Any takers on our buffalo wings, not quite as spicy as upstate New York, but pretty okay, I think."

"How many in an order?" Fred asked.

"Dozen per order."

"We'll take two orders of buffalo wings," Pat said.

"And do you know what you all want for dinnah?"

"Yes!"

"Okay, give it to me from the top." She looked at Popee first.

"Twin lobster dinner for me with cole slaw and fries." Popee turned to Pat and said, "How about you?"

"Make mine exactly the same," Pat said. He pointed to Zipper, who was sitting beside him.

"Me, too. That makes three identical orders," Zipper pointed to the person next to her, who happened to be Charles.

"No sense in changing the pattern; I'll take the same." He turned to Mom.

"Another, just the same for me, and add applesauce and an order of baby-size chicken nuggets for Carrie." Mom pointed to Fred.

"There begins to be a pattern," Fred said. "I'll take the twin lobsters, as big and mean as I can get them, cole slaw, and fries. How about you, big guy?" he said to Ralph, who was looking dreamily at Toni.

"Ah, whatever Fred said, okay with me," Ralph murmured.

"I should have ordered beef liver with onions," Fred said.

There was laughter. On trips away, Fred always told the boys he was going to take them to the "House of Liver."

"Sorry, sir," Waitstaff Hattie said, playing along with the obvious joke. "No liver served here on Mondays. And you, miss?" she said to Toni.

"I guess I'll have whatever this guy has," she said, pointing to Ralph.

"He's having two lobsters, cole slaw, and fries. Sound okay?" Hattie asked.

"Sure. He can show me how to eat a lobster. I've never had one before," Toni said.

Max could swear either T. L. Toni was blushing, had gotten sunburn, or she'd put on far too much makeup.

"Of course I will," Ralph purred.

Max thought his older brother sounded like some movie hero. He was pretty sure Ralph hadn't had many Maine lobsters himself. Tonight's dinner would be as much a learning game for him as it would be for T. L Toni, Charles, and himself.

Hatti looked very pleased. "I'll go get those appetizers. Lobsters will probably take 20 minutes. Enjoy outside. Explore around while these dinners are cooking. Take the side door over by the windows. You'll find another path to the shore, boiling room, and lobster pool," she said. She left to put the order in.

Charles was immediately up. Max followed him. Zipper followed Max.

"Looks like a grand exodus," Pat said. "Well, Zip's name is really Zepporah, wife of Moses . . . maybe they're on their way into the wilderness."

"If Zip played Zepporah, wife of Moses, then in this skit would Max be a modern-day Moses and Charles, Aaron?" Fred asked. "Suddenly we have vacation bible school."

"Oh, no. I put my foot down. The school year is starting soon enough. No, I veto this idea and opt we just enjoy our vacation," said Popee.

"Here! Here!" Pat said, raising his orange can of Moxie, Maine's state soda.

Meanwhile outside of the restaurant:

"Where are you going so fast?" Max said as soon as they were on the path.

"I want to see this pool. Do you think it's an Olympic-size one?" Charles asked. "I wonder if it's used for meets or just for swimming laps."

Max looked at Charles and then Zipper.

Zipper was grinning. She whispered in Max's ear: "Pool is where they keep lobsters. I doubt those mean crustaceans are in any mood for a race."

Max's reaction to her words was to buckle over laughing.

"Whaaa? What are you laughing about, Max?"

"It's a lobster pool, Charles. The lobsters will not be racing in any meet tonight," Max gasped. He coughed, wheezing, good thing he had an inhaler with him. He was laughing so hard he might have an asthma attack.

"Oh, okay," Charles said. "I wondered why I'd not read it in any information brochure I got on Eaton's Lobster Pool from . . . ."

"We know, we know, the Maine Visitors' Center," Max said.

"We only have a little time to explore. Let's not waste it," Zipper said.

They wandered through the lobster pool world watching as someone was cleaning mussels, another digging for clams, and to the far, far side and down a wobbly-looking, long walkway, men in a small rowboat were handing white buckets filled with very active lobsters to the men in charge of the cookers. They watched from a short distance as several lobsters were backward crawling up the insides of the buckets, only to be flipped back in by the experienced men in charge.

"See the little shed?" Zipper asked.

"Yep. Is it significant?" Charles asked.

"Very. Inside, someone takes lobsters from those buckets and fills customers' orders. Lobsters are put in number-marked bags; numbers match the orders. Then see there? Beside the shed, once-upon-a-time oil drums sit over wood coals. Steam is rolling out from the cover lids. That's where lobsters have their final bath. Then back into the shed where they're taken from bags, placed on trays, rushed to the kitchen to finish an order with fries, cole slaw, and hot melted butter."

They moved away. Even though lobsters were not especially cuddly, huggable creatures, still the two birthday boys would rather not watch them being dropped into the steaming bath.

Long grass grew high and wavy. Like dots on a map, someone had mowed places: spots with a picnic table and trash container for those who wished meals outside. And everywhere they looked there were flowers. On each picnic table, in Bell jars, fresh-cut flowers were placed. Other flowers grew in every whimsical way one could imagine.

"They get lots of large parties here. Class outings at the beginning and end of the school year . . . you know, those times when students can't sit still in stuffy classrooms even with all the windows open," Zipper told them.

"Oh, yeah. Especially when we've had a long winter with snow days, our teachers at home try to figure ways to make the last week or two of school meet the 180-day rule but in fun ways," Max said.

"Here, too. Teachers arrange with Eaton's to bring classes here for lunch. They work with the staff to make scavenger hunts. For example, the clues may read: 'Find a pink and pale blue lobster marker; look for the flowering apple tree . . . . on its fourth and lowest branch, you'll find a new clue.' Over there really close to the mud flat, see?" Zipper asked.

"The old rusty tractor?" Charles asked.

"Yes, that's the one. There's always a wooden box on its seat filled with slips of paper and on them clues to know where you'll find the next clue. When all clues are found, students return to collect rewards and have their lunch. And it's not lobster. Few children of fishing parents ever eat what vacationers want to eat. Eaton's staff makes treat lunches

124

minus lobster. Usually, sandwiches are made with what a teacher has told them are favorite homemade breads, served with fresh-ground peanut butter on one side and huge globs of Marshmallow Fluff on the other. And yep, always chips, a soda instead of milk, and ice cream: make-your-own-sundaes for dessert."

"Sounds decadent," Max said.

"Well, yep, it is a lunch filled with forbidden foods and drinks, but students spend the entire day, till nearly bus dismissal—teachers don't mind pumped-up-on-sugar students. Of course, parents have signed special permission slips," Zipper told them as they wandered around the wildland grounds.

Charles suddenly thought to check his watch. "Hey, I bet the appetizers have arrived and are being snatched and crunched by Ralph and T. L. Toni. We better hurry if we want any."

"Yep, and soon: crrrunch, smash, klunk, splish, whishing-whishing as lobster juices fly all around the table when anyone uses hammers and crunchers to battle their way into hard-shell lobsters," Zipper said. "It's very messy."

"That's okay, Zipper," Max told her "We're from Maryland, 'Land of Pleasant Living,' and steamed hot spicy crabs are very messy, too. And there people also get hit when crab juices fly."

Soon enough, the main meal was over, and all lobsters were reduced to piles of shell. Everyone had worn souvenir, plastic bibs, but still lobster juices, green fat, and butter had splashed on them, landing from the tops of heads to the tips of toes.

Before dessert, Hattie directed them to a hose for washing the worst of the mess off their hands.

For Max, Charles, and Zipper, the hands-down dessert choice was make-your-own sundae. They exited to that buffet where they were given a choice of ice creams by someone with scoopers. Next they had to choose strawberry or blueberry sauce, hot fudge, or caramel with whipped cream; last of all, assorted nuts, fruit, sprinkles, cherries, and other decorative toppings. The adults all felt full and lazy. In the case of Max and Charles, Fred and Pat had helped with the eating of the second lobsters, as the birthday boys' eyes had been far too big for their stomachs. The exception had been Zipper and Ralph, who helped Toni. Now, Mom, Popee, Pat, and Fred ordered from Hattie a slice of fresh blueberry pie heated, then decorated with scoop of vanilla ice cream, homemade whipped cream, and a cherry on top.

All declared it a wonderful meal. Everyone except Carrie, asleep on Mom's shoulder, thanked Hattie again and again for the best meal service ever.

While Fred and Pat paid the checks, Ralph and Toni added their initials and a heart in a discreet place on the wall; Zipper, Max, and Charles drew a "Kilroy was here" face, signed their names, and wrote the date.

They all staggered to truck and van. On the way home, they enjoyed the warmth of heaters on full blast. Outside the temperature had fallen to 49 degrees with a pink, red, and maroon sun setting. It was 8:35 p.m.

Back at the cottages, Mom and Popee announced: "Time to clean up and dress in winter clothes while Fred and Pat make a fire in the wood-burning stove. We'll meet up in the big cottage. Everybody bring comforters or heavy blankets with you. And those who went to The Cemetery, be ready to share the gravestone rubbings."

126

"We've a bit of time to warm up, but at 9:50 we'll head to the beach to see something very special," Mom told them.

When will it happen. . . . Max heard rumbling in his head. *Will it be during the day or will it be night?*

Chapter 9
A Cozy Fire and Messages on Gravestones. Oh???

O n sofa, chairs, footstools, rocker, and thick rug; with comforters around shoulders, as pillows, or resting over feet; bundled up lumpy warm, they all gathered by the crackling orange, yellow, blue flickering flames, which they watched through the wood stove's large glass panes. The blades of the fan revolved slowly, sending warm air away from the cathedral ceiling nooks and back down to the first floor.

"Wait until I tell my friends back home . . . we had a fire in a wood stove to warm us up on August 12," Toni said.

"That's just how it is some summer days and nights in Maine," Mom said.

"To those of you who were not with us," Pat said, "Zipper, Fred, Max, Charles, and I went on our hike where we found a private family cemetery. The stones are worn and some are broken and lying on the ground. They date back to the 1800s. Some only have names and dates. Some have messages, poems, and carved pictures."

"Yes," Fred added. "We saw carved pictures, which were very popular in the 1800s. But they were carved with a purpose, not just to make the stone pretty. During the1800s, grave carvings had symbols. Picture metaphors, if you will," Fred said.

"Like, what were these pictures of? What did they mean?" Toni asked. She was dressed in a new outfit. The clothes she wore to Eaton's Lobster Pool were soaking in the laundry room. Tonight, she was sensibly dressed in wool socks borrowed from Ralph, jeans and flannel shirt borrowed from Mom. Aunt Popee found an extra hooded sweatshirt and pair of hiking boots that just fit her.

"Great question, Toni. I did a study . . . actually found a few books on the subject of gravestones and the carvings and messages on them right here on the bookshelves in this cottage's library. I'll pass them out later. But now, with Fred's help, we'll read off a list of what might be carved on a gravestone and what it meant to those who saw it," Pat said.

"I'll name the symbol. Pat will tell you it's meaning in one or two words. We'll make this fast. Charles, count us down the way you do at home," said Fred.

"Got it. Here we go: 1 – for the Money. 2 – for the Show. 3 – To Get Ready. Aan-nnd 4—To Go!!!" Charles said.

Fred: "An anchor"   Pat: "Steadfast hope"
Fred: "Birds"   Pat: "Souls"
Fred: "Cherubs"   Pat: "Divine wisdom and justice"
Fred: "A broken column"   Pat: "Early death; a life ended too soon"
Fred: "A conch shell"   Pat: "Wisdom"
Fred: "Dolphin"   Pat: "Salvation"
Fred: "A lily"   Pat: "Purity"
Fred: "Hands"   Pat: "A relationship"
Fred: "Hearts"   Pat: "Devotion."
Fred: "Oak tree."   Pat: "Strength"
Fred: "Olive branch"   Pat: "Forgiveness"
Fred: "Poppy flower"   Pat: "Eternal sleep"
Fred: "Rooster"   Pat: "Awakening, courage"
Fred: "Rose bud"   Pat: "Love, hope, beauty on a child's

grave"

Fred: "A rose in full bloom"   Pat: "Love, hope, beauty of someone in their prime."
Fred: "Snake in a circle"   Pat: "Eternity, life"
Fred: "Tree Trunk"   Pat: "Beauty of Life"
Fred: "Weeping Willow"   Pat: "Mourning, grief"

"Done," Fred and Pat said together.

"Or at least that's as much as you've found so far. That's quite a list," Mom said.

"Yes, the short version," said Fred. "Some gravestones will have a little carved lamb on top. I saw one once but not today."

"Today we *did* see a schooner ship on one," said Charles, "but I didn't hear schooners mentioned on your list."

"I know, because this was only one list. There are many more lists and stories of the many symbols on stones. Something you should investigate, Charles, if you are interested. It would make a great independent-study history project. Okay, let's start with the stone you saw. Tell us about it."

"As Charles prepares to show us his rubbing, you'll notice it's rolled like a scroll," Fred said. "We rolled each rubbing as a way of protecting it. Remember, we were hiking."

Charles had used a navy blue crayon. The group looked and saw a schooner in full sail. It was sailing toward the right on gentle waves.

Charles read:

"Capt. David Billings d. July 23, 1883

Age 33 years and 8 months"

"And here is the message carved below," Charles read:

> "'Since thou can no longer stay
> To cheer me with thy love,
> I hope to meet thee again
> In your bright world above.'"

"Who do you think the speaker was in this message?" Pat asked.

"Maybe it's a message from his family. Did he have a wife and children?" Toni asked.

Toni? Toni's interested, thought Max. *Wow, this is not the Valley Girl Toni I always thought I knew. But maybe I didn't know her after all. Maybe I was judging her too quickly.*

"I have a rubbing that links Capt. David Billings to others," said Max. He unrolled his rubbing done with a dark purple crayon. "On it you will see a carving . . . ."

"Of a lily!" said Toni.

"Yes," said Max.

"And if you remember from what Pat just read to you..." Fred began.

"A lily means *purity*, right, Uncle Pat?" Zipper asked.

"Indeed it does."

"Let's see more," Toni said. "Max, unroll your scroll so we can see the rest of the carving."

"Here goes," said Max unrolling the paper, holding it top to bottom.

Ralph, sitting near Max, reached out and held the bottom for him so it wouldn't roll back but would stay open. Max thanked him and then read:

"Mellie, daughter of David and Hattie Billings
Died February 17, 1894,
17 years and 27 days old."

Toni said, "Oh, my. She has the same birthday as me, except I was born in this century. February 17, 1968."

"Another Hattie," Charles said. "Gosh. Max, Fred, and I met a Hattie over a year ago. And then we found letters in a trunk with the return address to Hattie. And then tonight, at Eaton's Lobster Pool, our waitstaff person was named. . ."

"Hattie," said everyone in the room except for Carrie.

"Why were so many women named Hattie?"

"Oh, well, Charles," said Popee. "Harriet was just a very popular name back then, and the popular nickname must have been Hattie."

"The message on this one is hard to read. In fact, without rubbing, it would be lost, I think," said Mom. "Read it to us, Max."

"My life has ended here, my dear ones,
But do not fear, or shed tears
For we will be united again.
I do not know when
For we shall meet again
But on that day,
We all shall be made one."

"Sad," Toni said, "Poor, poor girl."

"Sadder is this stone, I think," said Zipper. She unrolled her scroll, which revealed a rubbing done with a dark pink crayon:

"Anginett, daughter Capt. William S. Toothacher and
Lucy H. Toothacher died May 11, 1866, 2 years,

6 months and 2 days."

"Zipper, is there any symbol carved on her stone?" Pat asked.

"Yes, a weeping willow," said Zipper. "Symbol of mourning and grief."

"Right," said Pat.

"The majority of gravestones in this little graveyard were children of the Toothacher family, but was there any adult Toothacher?" Fred asked.

"Actually, I rubbed that stone, too," said Max. He unrolled another rubbing. On this one he had used a forest-green crayon. "No ship, just curling designs, but this is really a stone filled with important history." He read:

"In Memory of Capt. William S. Toothacher.

Who died in defense of our country in Richmond, Virginia, age 37 yrs. 6 mos. 2 days in 1865."

"The Civil War. Wow," said Ralph. "but did they bring his body all the way back here?"

"No, re-read it carefully: 'In Memory of'—in other words, it is a memorial stone. His body was left in Richmond," said Pat.

"But do you think they buried anything here?" asked Max. "Any of his personal things?"

"Perhaps," said Fred. "But it would take lots of searching through historical archives. Maybe something is said in a family letter or journal."

"I have the rubbing for a family member who lived a long but sad life," said Charles. He unrolled another paper. He'd done his rubbing with a red crayon. Immediately everyone saw flowers, ferns, and clearly carved words. They looked at the rubbing as Charles read:

"Lucy H. wife of William S. Toothacher, 1838-1910."

"She was the wife of the Civil War hero. And her husband and three of their daughters—Aginett, Melivia, and Lucy—died before she died. How sad," said Toni.

"And Hattie, who married Capt. David Billings, was a Toothacher, too. She must have been William's sister. On her grave we saw two hands reaching toward each other: Hattie's hand reaching to touch the hand of her beloved schooner captain husband, David Billings," said Fred.

"Real history. So much history in a little graveyard. The Toothacher family owned the farm where we hiked. We even saw the stone fences they built to keep cattle in. The descendants gave this land, over 100 acres, so it would always be preserved: a park where people could always hike," Fred said.

"Here are several more history books with photographs of tiny cemetery plots located on Deer Isle and Isle au Haut. You can look at them if you wish. We have a wee bit of time before bundling up and heading down to the shore," said Mom.

She handed out the old history books to those who put their hands up.

"Toni and I'll share," said Ralph, as he took one.

"Zipper and I will, too," said Max. "Um, if that's okay."

"Sure," said Charles.

But Zipper, seeing the book they'd been given, moved away. "Don't you and Aunt Popee need some help getting ready?" she asked Mom.

"Sure," said Mom.

"Come on, Zipper. You can help us get Carrie ready for her first experience seeing what an August night looks like," Aunt Popee added.

When she'd gone from the room, Charles whispered to Max, "Did that feel a bit odd to you? I mean, not wanting to look at the book with us?"

"Maybe she wanted to be helpful," said Max, but he also wondered why Zipper didn't want to look at pictures and read bits of text from a book about the history of Isle au Haut.

After reading the introduction, Max and Charles skimmed through the book until they reached photographs of stones:

The first showed a schooner and these words:
"Captain D. Eaton.
A Schooner ship sails on seas
Of storms and treasured memories.
Like a broken sword
Too soon, too soon
Taken away to shores unknown
Where battles were won, it was our loss.
When wild oceans tossed
His ship sank, all washed away,
Yet your soul will always be safe, we pray."

It was followed by another photograph of a stone that read:
"A Schooner ship sails on the seas
On stormy waves . . . and leaves us now
With only memories."

A few more pages, then they came to a photograph showing a grave. On its top was carved a baby lamb. It was for a baby girl and read:
"Born October 1 and Died October 1, 1801

A Stillborn
Your stillness
We will always remember."

"Well, that's really sad," Charles said, with a sigh.

They skipped through and then stopped at a photograph of a weeping willow; below was written:

"Sleep, dear one, sleep
Protected by willow boughs
We who are left behind
Kneel at your feet
And weep.
Yet we pray
To unite with you someday.
Sleep, sleep, sleep."

"Depressing stuff, these gravestones," said Charles, closing the book. "I'm going to go and make final preparations for the beach. You coming, Max?"

"In a minute." Max felt himself drawn to reopen the book and to look at all the pages until he reached the end.

Three pages from the last he found a photograph of a stone. It was undated. The carving was "the snake curled around, becoming a circle." Below, beside, and above the snake were beach roses in full bloom, then further down, a storm of crashing ocean waves. On the stone was a letter:

"Dearest Anna, gone from life
Spirit freed from flesh and strife.
I promise: Zepporah, our infant daughter,
Filled by memories shared,
Shall know her mother.
God's way, we do not understand.

Our love lives in these woodlands
Moss, trees, stones, here by this blue sea
And always it will surround what once was thee.
All my love, John."

It was a picture of the same gravestone he had seen today.

Max closed the book. He got up and went into the library. He hid the book on a shelf where Charles, Ralph, or not even Toni would ever find it. This was something he wanted to wonder about all by himself. He went back into the living room close to the heat-radiating wood stove. He curled up in one of the big, overstuffed chairs and stared at the flames.

In his thoughts he reviewed some of the questions that had haunted him all day, questions that were repeating now: *When will it happen? Has it begun today? Or will it really happen tonight?* And then the little haunting poem came back to him:

"Will it happen at sometime
Be it while the sun is bright
Or on a starry night?"

Chapter 10
Let the Meteor Shower Begin, and Then?
AND THEN?

To many onlookers, those beaming, bouncing flashlights moving along a narrow sandy pathway, through a blueberry barren, towards the beach, the vacationing Marylanders traveling must have looked like a caravan: all shapes, sizes, tall, short, bundled in comforters, some carrying deck chairs, a few acting as "light guides," shining flashlights for the others. They were, in fact: ages one year to forty-five, family and friends united, going toward water's edge, where they could enjoy the yearly sky show: the Perseid meteor showers.

The tide was perfect. It was slowly coming back in. There were many dry ledges to rest upon while staring into the blackest sky some in the group had ever seen.

"At home the glow of the malls and streetlights, the city 30 minutes away, lights in parking lots, at apartment and townhouse complexes, have taken away black night. Here we can easily see the Milky Way; back home we're lucky to find the Morning Star," Popee said.

"The Milky Way? I thought that was a candy bar," Toni said. "Like, that will be a big surprise to some of my friends at home."

At the beach they gathered close together in silence but minds were filled with questions. Finally, Charles asked: "What are our directions, Fred? Now we're here, what are we supposed to do?"

If someone had beamed a flashlight and haloed Fred's face, they'd have seen his smile and glittering eyes. "You're to find a spot, a comfy one. Better to be closer to the blueberry barren than down where barnacles, whelks, periwinkles, mussels, crabs, and clams might be something you crunch on. The ledges are flat. Some are huge, sloping down with lots of space for you to rest in comfort. There's plenty of room. Spread yourselves out. Make sure not to wander too far. This is a night for all us to share. Curl up in your comforters. Rest on your backs, and look straight up into this blackest of black skies. We're really lucky the moon is an 'eyelash' tonight."

"In the Greek myths, Perseus is the hero son of Zeus, greatest of gods. His mortal mother was Danae," said Popee.

"The Perseid meteor showers happen yearly. In the northeast, always around August 11 to 13. These meteor showers put on an amazing light show with as many as 50-80 meteors traveling horizontally across the sky and conveniently appearing in the evening. Many meteor showers other times in the year can be seen best between 2:00 and 4:00 a.m.," Pat said.

"Meteor shower? I'm not sure what exactly that is and what we'll be looking for?" Toni asked.

"Have you ever seen a falling star?" Charles asked her.

"Once or twice, I guess?"

"Well, tonight you'll have a chance to see between 50 and 80 of them . . . . in one hour," said Max. *Unless you're too busy necking with Ralph, that is,* he thought.

"Really! Wow, something else." Toni said. "Ralph, imagine all the wishes we can make."

"Hmmm?" said Ralph. "Oh, yeah. I guess."

Good ole Ralph, always the one who soaks in and doesn't say much. At least, that's what Mom has always hoped about him. But then, it must be true; he got into Harvard with mucho scholarships, Max thought. *Wonder what T. L. Toni sees in him, besides the fact*

*he's probably the most handsome guy Maryland Valley Girls have ever
seen outside of the movies.'*

"But what exactly are they?" Charles asked.

"Some call them 'comet rubble' . . . pieces of a comet
slamming through the Earth's atmosphere . . . Ready for this
fun fact?" Pat asked. "Some are moving at about 130,000
miles per hour."

"Fast!" Charles and Max said together. They laughed.

"They did it again. These two answering at the same
time; same little reaction answers, almost like twins," Mom
said laughing. "Max and Charles, our birthday boys, sorry, we
didn't give you a cake with candles to blow out this year.
Instead we brought you to a place where hopefully you'll see
many meteors or stars to wish upon."

"And here's two more really cool things to look for or, in
one case, look out for, though it is rare," Pat said.

"What?"

Pat's *"Look for"* got the attention of everyone in the
group, minus Carrie, who was contentedly chewing on a
teething ring.

"If Earth is passing through a really dense clump of
meteors, comet rubble, we'll see meteors with long-lasting
trails. They'll last a few micromoments longer than most
colorful trails, like a jet's smoke, but much better for many
reasons. I imagine tonight you might see trails that are blue,
yellow, orange, green as these meteors go whizzing across the
sky."

"Double wow," Charles said.

"And the danger?" Mom asked.

"The only real danger, which is very rare, sometimes bits
of an asteroid will fall: a meteorite. But those are really rare,"
said Pat.

"Are we safe? No one is going to get knocked in the head by pieces of a falling star?" Charles asked.

"Right," said Fred. "I think everyone will be okay."

"Now, scatter. Go find your viewing spot and start looking up. Pick a place, usually straight up, and start looking. Anybody need a flashlight? Or a flashlight guide?" Pat asked.

Everyone who needed a light guide was covered. Most everyone divided into small groups.

Charles, Max, and Zipper went back to the spot where they had met that morning, the place where they sat and talked before looking into the tidal pools. It seemed like the spot where they should be. *Almost like our beach home,* Max thought.

Soon excited voices were heard:

"There!"

"Did you see that?"

"Wow, what a trail . . . . long and blue!"

"They seem so close."

"Like right over you . . . like you almost want to duck. Whoa, there goes another!"

"Yellow trail here!"

"Oh, my! Like I'm making so many wishes I'm having to think. Help me, Ralph."

"Pat, Pat, have you made a wish?" asked Popee. "Have you made the one I've made?"

"Oh, Popee, Sweetie, many times and many times over," Pat said.

Max overheard them and wondered what they were making wishes for. Then he heard Mom say in a whisper, "A wish for a boy or a girl? I wonder if you two are making the same wish?"

Max heard Popee and Pat laugh. Pat whispered back, "I'll love either one, you know that. I wish for a baby big and healthy."

"Me, too," said Popee.

Wishes for either one. Wishes for big and healthy. I've heard these wishes before when Mom first knew she was pregnant with Carrie. I wonder. . . . No, I'm not wondering. I know. Zipper's Aunt Popee, Mom's friend who we always used to call Mrs. Sullivan, is going to have a baby. How great is that! They'll be super parents. How fun for Carrie to have a little friend, younger, but a little friend to play with, Max thought. He looked over to where Zipper was lying on the flat stone, body now almost completely wrapped in her big shaggy brown sweater.

"Hey, Zipper? Did you hear your Aunt Popee and Uncle Pat just now?"

Zipper turned and in the light of the starry sky, he could see her big dark, dark eyes. She was smiling one of her big, all-face smiles. "Yes," she whispered back. Her voice was very deep and almost gravel-like. "Yes, but I knew. Didn't they tell you? They will tonight when you get back. A little one born that they'll bring here next summer for me to see."

"I'm so happy for them," Max said. And he was. He knew Zipper's aunt and uncle had wanted a baby for a long time.

"Then make a wish for them, Max, on the very next most beautiful star you see tonight. All right?"

"I will, I promise. Oh, here's one now and with a lovely pink trail . . . . Perhaps it will be a girl," said Max, watching as the meteor flashed over what seemed to be the entire sky.

"Oh!"

"See!"

"Wow! Look. See? It's leaving a pink trail."

"How beautiful!"

"Make a wish!"

"Make a wish."

"Make a really important wish."

Meteors short, fast blazes of light. Meteors crossing inside and out, as if weaving, sewing the Big Dipper and Little Dipper together with their quick little lights. Meteors blazing from horizon to horizon across the sky. Meteors seemed only inches about their heads. And sound. The sounds sometimes heard; could that have been from these "wishing stars"? Or were they bay surf hushes against the shore sands?

Better than being at fireworks, Max thought. *Tonight, when most of us see amazing ones, we "Ahhhh!" and "Ohhh!" and "Wow!" the same way we do when we watch outstanding blooming fireworks displays. But this is more, much, much more. It's not a cylinder packed with a manmade display, gun powder with a fuse, lit by someone hiding in a safe place. It's Nature's all-natural, all-real show.* He couldn't keep his eyes away from the sky even when there was a lag time between meteors; looking at the Milky Way was a show in itself.

Then Max felt a shifting by his side. Zipper had moved closer to where he was. In the night light, he saw she was standing, bending near to him.

"Hey, listen. Take this," she said, taking his hand and putting something in it. A paper envelope. "Put it in your pocket for now. Don't lose it, promise?"

"Oh, sure it'll be safe," Max took the envelope and wedged it far down into his front jeans pocket. "It's at the very bottom of my pocket. No safer place than that. I'll keep it safe for you."

"Good. Thanks," Zipper said in that same gravelly voice.

Max could see she was wearing the sweater wrapped tightly around her: up to her chin, down to her feet, falling down, even covering her fingers. Over the sweater, her long hair flowed as it had looked at dawn that morning when he first saw her sitting on the same big stone.

"I must speak to Aunt Popee and Uncle Pat," Zipper said.

"Okay," said Max. "Later."

"Yes," Zipper said softly. "Later, Max."

He watched her go to her Uncle Pat and Aunt Popee. Then heard someone say:

"Look! WOW! Look at that one!"

Max watched as a huge meteor blazed across the sky. It seemed only inches above them. Its trail was the longest ever: blue-blue, ocean blue with sparkles, like when the sun shines on the waves making all a glittery, shimmering, glimmering bright, so bright you almost couldn't look; so bright you must shade our eyes. That's how bright this meteor was; bright as sunlight flecks alive on dark, dark water.

"Oh, the best ever!" Max heard Charles say.

"I will never ever forget it, will you?" Toni asked Ralph.

"No, never, ever," he said softly.

"It's very late," Fred said.

"Yes, I need to get Carrie in bed. And tomorrow will be another day," Mom said. "There's much more to see and do."

Max could hear Mom and Fred beginning to gather and pack things they'd carried down.

"And tomorrow night, if the night is clear like it is tonight, there'll be meteors and maybe as many as tonight . . . one never knows," said Pat.

Max heard everyone gathering chairs, comforters, yawning, beginning to walk back up the sandy path.

144

Charles came by his side, flashlight on and also the beam of his watch. "It's 10:00, Max. I guess we're born," Charles said. It was a family joke. Each birthday, at the hour, minute, of a birth (when it was known), someone, or all, would pick that exact moment to wish another happy birthday.

"Guess we better go and get our hugs from Mom . . . and Fred," Max said.

Max and Charles went to Mom and Fred for birthday group hugs, happy wishes, and they each endured Mom's "French style" kiss—right cheek, left cheek.

"We actually do have cake up at the cottage with 21 candles ready to be lit, then blown out," Mom told them.

"Oh, Mom, we knew you wouldn't disappoint us," said Charles.

Max looked around. Everyone had gone from the beach, heading on the trail back to the cottages. Everyone gone. It was very dark. The surf was loud. The tide was coming closer and closer. Soon where they'd been sitting would be covered by swirling, salty, cold bay waters.

***

No one was up. Max was alone in the cottage library. One light was lit. It was now, only now, he felt ready to reach deep into the front pocket of his jeans. To reach down low and retrieve the envelope Zipper had given to him, to open it, now with no one around. *Maybe it will explain,* he thought.

At the cottage when the cake with 21 candles had been brought out, and the "Happy Birthday" song had been sung, one person wasn't there. One person he'd met for the first time that day . . . one special person was missing. Maybe the envelope would have a note inside explaining why.

145

He pulled the envelope out, opened it, and found the note. He read it, then carefully he put it back in the envelope, back in his pocket.

"Dear Max,

      I will appear here on this beach
when you least expect.

      I will come back when I can.
I too do not know when

      But I will.

Look for me on the low or high tides,

      in the surf song periwinkles love,
the call of the dove, sea stars,

      and when stars glow colors across the skies.
Your friend,

                        Zepporah (Zipper)

Epilogue

The coast of Maine has been a summer destination for centuries. It is said that the early American Indian tribes would travel out of thick woodlands and camp on the shoreline where they'd gather food from the sea. They dried and smoked fish, clams, mussels, preserving for later meals this bountiful plenty. When midsummer arrived, bringing ripe, sweet berries, many were picked, nibbled, dried, and packed: early fruit wraps to be enjoyed come winter. After the warm summer sun and breezes turned into clouds with colder winds, the first peoples returned to their woodland homes lugging bundles of all they had gathered.

In the late 1600s early European settlers arrived in Maine, seeking a new beginning. Little villages were built around the Meeting House. Later, in the late 1800s, people from big cities like Philadelphia, New York, Boston, Baltimore, and others, travelled by train and schooners, then over earthen roads in carriages, wagons, and later motor cars, to summer cottages built near balsam forests, on the granite ledges and sandy shores in Downeast Maine.

As many have discovered for hundreds of years, a vacation in Maine always begins with a journey from where you live to this special place, far away.

***

Today, Deer Isle, Maine, is still very much the way it was on August 12, 1985.

You still must cross The Bridge to arrive on Little Deer Isle, then go around The Causeway to be on Big Deer Isle. You still must climb the tall, tall hill.

Paradise is unchanged and if you go there, plan on seeing it at high tide. The Preserve with hiking trail is carefully taken care of and open to the public, only the color of the blazes has changed from blue to red. And yes, there is a stonewall, which may need a stone put back. There is also the family cemetery.

In the village, you can still have Gifford's ice cream and then cross the quiet street and shop at The Periwinkle. Though you may not be waited on by Miss N., you can buy many made-in-Maine books, shirts, cards, things made out of wood, and enjoy penny candy, even Fireballs.

The Lily Pond is still filled with lilies white and gold and many little fish: minnows, sunfish, bass, brown, and brook trout are there. Bull frogs "tunk" on the left side of the pond and the beach is waiting for sand castles to be made. If you are older, you can walk around the left side and find a rope: the Tarzan swing.

The Deer Isle beaches are unchanged: wild and sandy, filled with tidal pools, where there are many whelks, periwinkles, and hermit crabs. Sea stars have been missing for a few years, but marine biologists report they will be coming back. And yes, as I write this, they are yellow, purple, big, and small.

The Island Nursing Home is still a place where little children go for day care, and yes, special shows bring elders and the very young together. If you stop in, you'll probably see a cat walking down a hall, or a visiting dog being read to. Maybe even a few birds are in cages ready to chat with you.

Eaton's Lobster Pool is closed and will not reopen. The cottages where Max, Charles, Popee, Pat, and all the rest stayed are now privately owned.

And Zepporah, Zipper, Zip—will she be there? That I cannot answer. Nor can I tell you who she is or where she went the night of August 12, 1985. But there are many stories told, when you visit Down East Maine, of sailors who've seen girls and women who are mysterious swimmers with huge dark eyes and wonderful smiles. Some stories even have given them a name. They call them *selkies*.

Is the Zipper you have just read about a selkie?

Well, I believe this is a mystery for you to decide.

About the Author

Susan Yaruta-Young is a published poet and short story crafter who enjoys writing for all ages in all genres. She was a Maryland State Arts Council Poet in the Schools from 1974-1996. In 1996, Susan and her husband, Luther Young, left their small farm in Baltimore County to move their family to Downeast Maine. A graduate of Bangor Theological Seminary, she has served as a pastor at several small Maine churches.

Made in the USA
Middletown, DE
21 September 2016